New

THE GIFTS OF JIMMY V

A Coach's Legacy

THE GIFTS OF JIMMY V

A Coach's Legacy

Bob Valvano

TRIUMPH
B O O K S
CHICAGO

Library of Congress Cataloging-in-Publication Data

Valvano, Bob.
  The gifts of Jimmy V : a coach's legacy / Bob Valvano.
    p. cm.
  Includes index.
  ISBN 1-892049-30-9
  1. Valvano, Jim. 2. Basketball coaches—United States—Biography.
  I. Title.

  GV884. V34 V35 2001
  796.323'092—dc21
  [B]   2001047014

This book is available in quantity at special discounts for your group or organization. For further information, contact:
  Triumph Books
  601 South LaSalle Street
  Suite 500
  Chicago, Illinois 60605
  (312) 939-3330
  Fax (312) 663-3557

Printed in the United States of America

ISBN 1-892049-30-9

Interior design by Amy Flammang

Photo insert design by Patricia Frey

To Darlene

CONTENTS

FOREWORD

SINCE WE WON THE NCAA CHAMPIONSHIP IN APRIL OF 2001, I HAVE been inundated with requests for various projects. Don't get me wrong: I hope I am inundated every year for as long as I keep coaching. That's what happens when you win, and that is fine with me.

But as you will read in the pages that follow, perhaps I learned a bit from watching Jim Valvano trying to deal with everything that came his way after he won the NCAA championship. He and I discussed this, among the hundreds of other things we talked about. He told me, "Mike, you have everything going for you right know. I have some advice: don't $%#& it up."

I have tried to take that to heart, and so I have been very careful with the great many things that have come my way. However, while I have turned down offers to do forewords for other books, I was honored to do this one.

You see, Jim Valvano was my friend.

Jim and I played against each other, he at Rutgers, me at Army. When he was coaching at Iona, I was coaching at Army, and we competed again. And, of course, we competed in the ACC as well, starting in the same year, 1980. Because of that, it was never easy for Jim and me to be close during those years, although I think we got along pretty well. But when he got out of coaching, our friendship grew greatly and we looked back at many of our similar experiences. It got to be a very tight relationship, one based on very unique and yet shared backgrounds.

Anyone who coaches at the ACC level knows it's pretty hard. You don't take success for granted, and you are rightfully proud when you succeed. Jim had great success at this level. He should and will be remembered as a fine coach, and he went on to be a very good broadcaster as well.

Those stories are interesting ones, and worth telling, but this book focuses on something else—not on Jim's achievements, but on who he really was. That ultimately will be what we remember most of all.

Like many of the people in this book, my life was touched by Jim's, and I will always greatly value the time we spent together, especially during the last months of his life, when he was at Duke Hospital. It was then that he asked me to be a part of the last team he would form, the team that comprises the V Foundation for cancer research.

I think it is his greatest team.

It is one of the many ways that Jim's spirit lives on, and where the people whose lives he touched are able to try to make a difference in ways that Jim would have done himself.

It is important to me that a portion of the proceeds from this book will go to the foundation as we work towards finding a cure for this terrible disease. In fact, there is only one thing I wish for more than once again having the opportunity to compete against Jim on the sidelines. That is to have him here with us when we find that cure for cancer. I would like to share that moment with my friend and let him know that he inspired many in that fight.

Enjoy the stories about Jimmy V.

— Mike Krzyzewski
June 2001

PREFACE

WHY THIS BOOK?

Several reasons, but the most compelling for me, not necessarily in order of importance, are: an exchange of letters with an ESPN Radio listener, a tale involving Babe Ruth, a pregame talk by former Rutgers and Duke coach Bill Foster, and a story from the 1981 North Carolina State season.

First, the letters.

As part of my nightly program on ESPN Radio, I told listeners that I'd love to hear any personal stories they had about my brother that they would be interested in sharing for this book. Jim did a lot of public speaking, was a high-profile coach and broadcaster for nearly 20 years, and interacted with many, many people in the course of his career. Still others who never met him were moved by speeches they saw on TV or by articles they read that quoted him. I wanted to share some of those stories in this book, and asked people to send them to me. The following was one of the responses:

> I heard about this on ESPN Radio last night. My take on Valvano is probably not something you'll want to see in the book.
>
> From the start of the "sanctification" of Valvano (the "V Foundation"), I've been befuddled by all the attention this man has received. He ran one of the dirtiest programs in college basketball . . . in fact, Tarkanian is a choirboy by comparison. Why do today's society and the media try to raise up such poor examples for people to look up to?

My dad always told me that there are only two things in life that can't be taken from you . . . your honesty and integrity. Only you can give those away. I don't know when Valvano gave his away, but I'd bet he wouldn't recognize either, it was so long ago. Was his death tragic? For his family and friends, no doubt. For the rest of us, no. There are many people that lead honorable lives who pass from view and memory with little or no fanfare that would make better examples for everyone, Valvano included.

I know this book is going to be used to help charitable foundations of one sort or another, so maybe some good will come from Valvano's life and passing. I hope it's successful.

Gary Riggle

The following was my response:

Mr. Riggle:

I appreciate the kind words about your wishes for the book, and very much appreciate your candor about my brother and his reputation. Your summation is in fact one of the main reasons I want to write the book.

I agree that he has been "sanctified" and it is for the wrong reasons. He got sick and died very young, and handled it with great dignity and courage. I am proud of that. But he really was no different in his illness than he was in health. It was simply the perception, publicly, that changed, and your comments are a reflection of that.

Let me ask you a question. You say Jim ran one of the dirtiest programs in America. Did you know that after three investigations, the only thing he was ever accused of was that his players sold complimentary athletic shoes and tickets? Period. Did you know that? Did you know that the guy who ran the NCAA investigation, Dave Dideon, a hardened veteran of dealing with slick, underhanded coaches, said that he never investigated a more misunderstood coach than Jim, and that following the investigation, he wrote a letter to Jim saying that if he had a son, he would be proud to have him play for Jim? Probably not, and my guess is that if you did, you would rather not have it cloud your preconceived judgment that Jim was a bad guy.

He made mistakes. He tried to do too many things at once. He assumed details were being tended to that weren't, that he should have seen to. But dirty program? Astoundingly inaccurate, but perpetuated, as is the misconception that he became a "good guy" when he got sick. He was always a "good guy," an inspiring guy, and he made his share of mistakes. Both have been blown out of proportion, and it makes Jim a cartoon character.

Please don't take my remarks personally . . . I am probably tilting at windmills to think I will change anyone's mind, but it is a noble fight. To fight it, I can't, and won't, make Jim out to be a saint, but the criticisms are as inaccurate as the accolades are simplistic.

It is worth trying.

Bob Valvano

Now, about the Babe.

My friend Andy Pollin, who among other things is Tony Kornheiser's sidekick on his ESPN Radio show, once visited a class I was teaching at St. Mary's College. The course was "The Sociology of Sport," and the topic was the changing role of the sports media. Pollin shared this story:

> A group of sportswriters was traveling by train with the New York Yankees, and were playing cards in the parlor car late into the evening. Suddenly down the aisle came a woman running, her clothes in obvious disarray as she hastily made her way through the car. A few moments later, down the aisle on the run comes the Bambino himself, in pursuit that would have made Lawrence Taylor proud.
>
> The writers don't even look up. One finally says, "It would make a great story. . . ."

And obviously, it is a story that, in that era, would not be repeated, at least in the media.

So much has changed since then. Today it seems that you cannot be considered a serious writer unless you unearth some embarrassing personal transgressions on the part of your subject. Regardless of the nature, and in some cases even the truthfulness, of the allegations, as long as they portray the subject unflatteringly it lends a certain "seriousness" to the writing.

As I indicated earlier, I want this to be a serious look at Jim and how he went from being a skinny kid with a bad sinus condition to become a national figure who inspired and touched many lives. Some not so flattering things are in this book. Jim made some mistakes, as we all do, and some of those mistakes are included here. I want to try to help you get to know Jim as I did, and it's difficult if not impossible to relate to a character who's portrayed only in a favorable light. I'll try to paint the picture "warts and all," as Oliver Cromwell is said to have instructed his portrait painter.

I'll take care in doing this, because a writer can skew any story to imply something that's inaccurate or magnify a shortcoming inappropriately. Case in point, regarding Bill Foster. One of the finest coaches and gentlemen the college game has ever known, he was way ahead of his time in terms of preparation, organization, and efficiency. So if I shared just this one story with you—a true story—I would be painting the most inaccurate of pictures.

When Jim was playing for Coach Foster at Rutgers, they had just gone through one of their typical detailed pregame preparations, the crux of which was the zone defense that Rutgers had prepared just for that game. They had practiced it, drilled it, and spent the majority of the pregame talk discussing it.

As Jim was headed out to the court for the opening tip, Coach Foster beckoned him. Jim quickly returned to the sideline.

"Jim," Coach said, "who's your man?"

Jimmy looked puzzled, then responded, "Coach, we're opening zone, remember?"

"Oh, that's right," Coach Foster responded.

Rutgers, well prepared and well coached, used the zone effectively to win that game. However, if all I told you was that pregame story (with slanted editing at that) I could easily create in your mind the impression of a confused or unprepared, rather than a momentarily distracted, Coach Bill Foster. This, as I said earlier, is not only inaccurate, but is exactly the opposite of the truth.

That's the fine line I have to try to walk in this book. I'll be using true stories that paint an accurate picture of who Jim really was, but I make no apology for leaving out stories that are open to misinterpretation or serve no purpose in defining Jim or describing how he touched so many lives.

Now the North Carolina State story.

In the 1980–1981 season, N.C. State was playing the University of Virginia, led by All-American, 7'4" center Ralph Sampson. Jim, the head coach at N.C. State, devised a defensive game plan that had his team playing a tight 2-3 zone. One of the special twists devised just for Sampson was that the back defensive man on his side, in this case Scott Parzych, was instructed not to go out into the corner in the zone defense as he normally would, but to stay packed in tight, helping double cover Sampson. This was emphasized throughout the preparation: "Don't go to the corner. Whatever you do, don't go to the corner!"

The game was tight throughout: intense, close, and hard fought. Inevitably, as the game wore on, Parzych started going out to the corner defensively. Every chance he got, Jim would yell at Parzych as he ran by the bench, "Scott, stay in . . . stay in!" But Parzych kept drifting out to the corner.

Finally, there was a momentary stop in play to inbound the ball about 15 feet from the Wolfpack bench. The assistants saw an exasperated Jim Valvano leap up and race over to Parzych to get in his face. Play resumed and Jim returned calmly to the bench, where an assistant, who couldn't help noticing the transformation, asked him what had happened.

"I asked him why he kept going to the corner," Jim said, "and Scott said to me, 'Coach, I *gotta* go to the corner.'"

Puzzled, the assistant said, "So what did you tell him?"

"I said, 'So go,'" Jim replied.

Such is the case here.

Jim's successful playing career, and to a greater degree his coaching career in the spotlight of the Atlantic Coast Conference, will be of interest to many. His controversial dismissal at the end of his N.C. State tenure is fraught with interesting stories and personalities. His broadcast career shot across the media sky like a meteor, bright but all too brief. And his emotional battle with cancer, and his inspiring message when he was literally at death's door, touched millions of people across the nation.

But for me there is a more compelling reason to write this book. I just gotta go to the corner and tilt at peoples' minds to correct some of the many misconceptions, good and bad, concerning my brother, Jim Valvano.

And I can hear Jim saying, "So go."

1

THE GIFT

LET ME TELL YOU ABOUT JIM VALVANO. I CAN DO SO FROM A UNIQUE perspective, because I can say with absolute certainty that I am the only little brother he ever had. Thank you. Hold the applause until all the names have been read.

Why that should make one a celebrity of sorts, I don't know, but it does. ("Hey honey, you'll never guess who I met today. Connie Chung's aunt's cousin!") We all do it, and I don't mind it, because whenever someone makes a fuss about "Jim Valvano's brother" it keeps Jim alive for me in a small way. More than that, it reminds me that he touched so many lives while he was on this earth, and continues to touch them today.

People constantly tell me that Jim Valvano moved them. They usually cite one of three things: (1) the 1983 National Championship game against Houston, where North Carolina State pulled what many consider one of the biggest upsets in NCAA history; (2) one of the hundreds of motivational speeches he gave to businesses and organizations around the country; and (3) his unforgettable ESPY speech two months before his death, with its stirring exhortation, "Don't give up. Don't ever give up!" His ability to motivate, inspire, excite, and move people was simply extraordinary. It's difficult to explain, although that's what I want to attempt to do in this book. And, as Jim would be the first to tell you, it really is a gift.

That's how we arrived at the title of this book, which, however, in itself is a bit misleading. The title should be *The Gift My Father Gave Me*, and the author should be Jim himself. He always said that our father, Rocco Valvano, gave him the greatest gift any one person can give to another—the gift of believing in yourself because the other person believes

1

in you. Jim always claimed that whatever success he had, and for that matter whatever success anyone enjoys, can at some point be traced to a person who simply said, "I believe in you. I believe you can do this."

Based on the reactions of people to this message, I would say most agree. I know I agree, and believe whatever I have been able to achieve is in large measure because my father—and my whole family—believed in me and supported me. But I had a secret weapon. I had Jim, who took the gift my father gave him and not only passed it on but multiplied it, supercharged it, and made its positive message a catalyst that propelled countless people to success in different fields of endeavor.

You'll meet a good number of those people in this book. In fact, that is one reason for its existence: to celebrate the achievements of the many people for whom Jim played an inspirational role. In so doing, my hope is that you may be inspired too.

I coached basketball for 20 years and know what it is to be able to move and motivate those around you. Many people are in positions where they are responsible for being a catalyst every day, and it is challenging, fulfilling work. It's also not always easy. As Jim used to ask all the time, "Who motivates the motivators?" Perhaps this book will help in that regard, by reminding you that you can—we all can—make differences in our communities in ways we may not even realize.

One of Jim's favorite quotations was "Every day ordinary people do extraordinary things." I know he believed it, and lived it, and loved that sentiment for many reasons. Jim believed in taking what you *do* seriously, but not taking *yourself* too seriously. Isn't that what that quotation is all about? We're all just ordinary people, and there's no reason to get too hung up on ourselves, but we can all do great things. "Dream, work, believe"— that was Jim's mantra. The excitement of knowing you may have greatness within, and the knowledge that someone *believes* that you do: that was the essence of Jim's message.

Strangely though, while we all say we understand why it is so important, and we all think it is something we should do for the people in our lives, many of us don't inspire others as often as we would like. Why is that? Why don't we do it better? That is another reason for this book. We can examine the gift Jim Valvano gave me and so many others, and figure out how we can keep it in our lives and pass it on.

It's a magical gift. You can give it all away to someone else, and still have all of it left for yourself! How many things in life can you do that with? Isn't that amazing? You certainly can't do that with material things. But that's the best part about this gift: you can give it away and keep it at the same time, and it enriches both you and the person receiving it.

What's the catch? Well, like many things "magical," there's more to it than might appear at first glance. This gift is not always easy to get, to find, or to maintain, no matter how much we might wish it were. Which leads us back to the first sentences of this chapter. I must tell you about Jim Valvano, the complex, emotional, street smart, naïve, caring, gruff, loving, competitive, compassionate, multidimensional, misunderstood man in order for anything about his "gift" to make sense. That won't always be easy. Jim had more colors than a rainbow, and could change his mind like Sinatra changed his clothes. Which is to say, often.

While changing his mind could sometimes lead to accusations of Jim being calculating, disingenuous, insincere, and shifty, many times it was nothing more than him simply saying, "Hey, I changed my mind." The frequency and alacrity with which people reacted to this leads me to think that nobody must change their minds anymore. And that's sad. If you think you have all the answers, you stop trying to learn, and if you do that, you stop trying to grow, and then, quite simply, you die.

That's a huge part of Jim's message, and one he lived literally until he himself died. Sure there was a great deal of courage in what Jim did in the last months of his life, but at the core was his faith in the knowledge that even at that point he was asked to make, and did make, a choice. He chose to continue to learn, and change, and grow, and live, living the gift his father gave him, believing that even in his last days he could do great and worthwhile things.

And he did. Oh, did he ever. I contend he did more in his last 11 months than many of us do in our entire lives. Somewhere in those painful, frightening, final months, while the cancer was eating away his body, there was a little voice, the voice that contained the gift from my father, which was still telling Jim that there were important things to be done, and that someone believed he was able to do them.

Jim Valvano was a man of contradictions. He often appeared cocky, but was frequently insecure. He could be flamboyant one moment and remarkably reserved the next. He loved his family, yet spent a great deal of time away from home; believed in academics, yet recruited subpar students; wanted a shot clock, yet played a game where neither team scored 40 points. Critics will say, "See, he stood for nothing!"

That is my last reason for writing this book. We all deserve criticism, and Jim is no exception. But the seeming contradictions, the changes of mind, the inconsistencies, these are what make any of us—*all* of us—human. But what lies underneath is who we really are, and Jim's beliefs, those instilled by the gift our father gave us and all that it encompassed, were rock solid all his life. They were why he achieved what he achieved, why he made such an impression on the lives he touched. They were so powerful that the destructive forces of cancer were no match for them. It is why one ordinary man achieved so many extraordinary things.

As Jim said, "Cancer can take away all my physical abilities . . . but it cannot touch my mind, it cannot touch my heart, it cannot touch my soul . . . and those things are going to live on forever."

And they do. So let's begin . . . at the end.

2

GOOD-BYE

I JUST SAT AND LOOKED AT HIM. MY BROTHER. MY HERO, MY IDOL, MY friend. He was the man who had played with me when I was a little kid, protected me and looked after me in my adolescence, helped me in my career, made me laugh longer and harder than anyone I had ever known, and given me enough magical, one-of-a-kind experiences to last more than a lifetime. I loved him as much as it's possible for a brother to love a brother.

And I wished with all my heart that he would die.

We were in the Duke University Hospital Oncology Unit. Jim's wife, Pam, their three daughters, Nicole, Jamie, and Lee Ann, and my mother, Angela, were all there. My brother Nick had gone back to his hotel room to shower and was due back any moment. My wife, Darlene, and my three-year-old son, Nicholas, were also due to arrive shortly. I had arrived back in North Carolina myself only a short while earlier, after a chaotic couple of days.

I had left for home the day before, having spent a few days visiting Jim in the hospital. I took Amtrak back to Washington from Raleigh, using the long train ride to settle my mind and jangled emotions. Jim, who just eight weeks earlier had given that emotional speech at the ESPYs in New York, had deteriorated steadily from that point on. In truth, he was not in very good shape even then. Those who saw him earlier in the day in New York didn't believe that he could even make it up on the stage that night, much less move everyone the way he did with his lively, funny, spirited speech.

As I look back on it now, it's easy for me to see that I was in complete denial during those eight weeks. I knew he was very sick and that the prospects were bleak. But I kept looking for some kind of rally, some improvement that, while it might be temporary, would nevertheless be a bright spot for all of us. I envisioned "the end" as something down the road, something that, to be sure, would have to be dealt with, but not till some far-off point in the future.

If that sounds vague, it should. That's what denial is like. Specifics are rarely good, so you just avoid them. I knew Jim might die from this cancer (might!), but wherever we were, I thought we weren't there *yet*.

So, after a couple days' visit, I said good-bye, got on my train, and headed back to D.C. I had no more than reached Union Station when I found out that Pam had called my wife, telling her that there wasn't much time left, and if I wanted to see Jim again, I should turn right around and go back to North Carolina. I headed right to National Airport and took the next flight to Raleigh.

I was incredulous. I knew Jim was bad, but the day before he had said to me, "You come back soon, now." I promised I would, thinking it would be in a couple of weeks, and even daring to hope I might see some improvement then. It had been an odd visit, to say the least. Jim had been going through various stages of illness that ranged from disconcerting to downright terrifying. He slept through terrible spasms in his limbs, almost like an epileptic seizure—violent shakes that we were helpless to stop or control. Fellow coach Mike Krzyzewski came in for his daily visit during one of these times, and I could see the shock on his face.

That's the thing about cancer. No matter how bad you think it is, it always has another sinister surprise in store. Each time we resigned ourselves to the new parameters of Jim's life, his disease would change the rules on us and make new, more disgusting and repulsive demands. Then all of us, led by Jim himself, would try to figure out how to adjust to the new set of circumstances.

Jim fought the cancer just as he coached, always looking for a new way to get the job done. Always battling. Late in his illness he couldn't see clearly out of one eye, a problem that blurred and doubled his vision. No problem. He didn't complain. He just sat there with one eye closed tight, looking like Popeye, but laughing with me while we watched *Whose Line Is It, Anyway?* on TV. Jim's enthusiasm for that show quickly rubbed off on me, and it's still one of my favorites.

Still, that last visit had easily been the most disturbing one yet. His speech had become so slurred that it was difficult to understand anything he said, and much of the time he was basically incoherent. In fact, with the exception of encouraging me to return soon, he had not had a moment of lucidity in my presence the entire day—with two notable exceptions.

The first was an incident his daughters and I still laugh about. We had been keeping our normal bedside vigil, watching Jim drift in and out of consciousness and occasionally mutter something incomprehensible. Suddenly and without warning, he shot straight up in his bed, pointed to his daughters, and said "Out!" as clear as can be. Apparently the one thing able to call him back to full alert was impending bedpan duties, which had to be performed by someone. He was determined it wasn't going to be his daughters.

The second moment will stay with me forever.

That last night, before getting on the train back to D.C., Jamie and I spent the night at the hospital so Pam could get some much-needed rest. Jim was gesturing and trying desperately to talk, but by now he was so hopelessly indecipherable that it broke my heart. Suddenly I remembered that when my father-in-law had Alzheimer's disease, until the very late stages he always responded positively to music, especially old, familiar tunes.

When I was four years old, Jim and I shared a bedroom in our home in Seaford, Long Island. I'm sure this must have just thrilled him, being 15 years old. But it was a three-bedroom house, and Nick, our oldest brother, got his own room. *C'est la vie.* Jim, as far as I can remember, was pretty good-natured about it. What I specifically recall is that he was always singing. Not in the choir, or in the school glee club, but in our bedroom, in the shower, around the house, in the car, everywhere, all the time. Sing, sing, sing. Benny Goodman would have loved him. And he wasn't timid about it, either. None of this humming a tune under his breath. He sang loudly, robustly, with gusto and enthusiasm, and didn't care who heard him. He took Thoreau's adage, "The woods would be silent if only the best birds sang," very much to heart. There was no danger of the woods being silent when Jim was around. Jim decided to teach his four-year-old kid brother two songs, both Sinatra hits. One was "Would You Like to Swing on a Star?" and the other was "High Hopes."

On that impossibly sad April night at Duke University Hospital I decided to sing those songs to my brother. I launched into the first one. With dawning awareness, Jim struggled to sit up in bed as a lucid, happy smile came across his face. In a clear voice, he started to sing too. Loudly. Then Jamie joined in, and even though we were unsure of some of the words, Jim kept us going. I hadn't sung it much since I was four, and couldn't remember all the animals mentioned, but that was no problem for Jim. "High Hopes" was next, and though we were all a bit fuzzy on those words, what we lacked in precision we more than made up for in volume and enthusiasm. My brother, Jamie's dad, was back, albeit briefly.

That's the last time I feel I really saw Jimmy.

Now I was back in that hospital sickroom after my quick turnaround, and I myself felt like I was going to be sick. We had spent the better part of the day watching Jim stare blankly at the ceiling, breathing laboriously. I noticed that the monitor, which had been attached to the oxygen mask, had been removed from the room. Not a good sign. Over the days and weeks we had watched the numbers on that monitor carefully, having been warned that if they dropped below a certain level, we should call the desk immediately. The monitor's absence told me all I needed to know about what the numbers would have been and how dire the situation really was.

It was hard to look at Jim's wide-eyed, blank stare. I was no longer in denial. I knew where we were. And so after days of grotesque spasms, labored breathing, incoherence, and that blank stare, all of which followed months and months of excruciating, scream-triggering pain, I knew it was close to being over, and I wanted out. For Jim, for his family, and for me. Definitely for me. So I looked at this man whom I loved so much, and in my helplessness and desperation, all I could think was . . .

Die.

Please. I know you are not coming back, so please go. I even talked to him and said that. I knew he couldn't respond, and wasn't sure he could understand, but I put my mouth close to his ear and whispered, "It's OK, Jim. You can go. We'll take care of Pam and the girls . . . they'll be fine. You can let go now . . . it's OK. I love you. . . ."

I was wracked with all the sadness that anyone watching suffering endures, but added to that was the thought that all I could do for my brother, this man who had done so much for me, had helped me in so many ways large and small, was to wish for his death.

I was distracted for a moment by a commotion in the small visitor's room down the hall. My wife and son had arrived, and as the youngest grandchild, there was much fussing over Nicholas. My mother went up the hall to see him, as did his three cousins. Pam stayed with Jim, and after greeting my beautiful son, I came back into the room with Darlene. Soon Nicole would return as well. Just the four of us sat around the bed as I stared at his battered and beleaguered figure for the last time. He was 47 years old, but after the ravages of the disease had taken their toll he looked to be about a hundred.

But a man's life is measured not only by a span of years. There is also its impact on the lives of others. By this measure, Jim Valvano lived not 47 years, or one hundred years, or one thousand; he continues to live in those who knew him.

3

CORONA

IF THE FOUR WORDS THAT CAME TO DEFINE JIM VALVANO'S LIFE WERE "I believe in you," the four that defined both his and our older brother Nick's childhoods were, "Take your brother along." Like Mary's little lamb, everywhere that Nicky went little Jimmy was sure to go.

And there were a lot of places to go in Corona, New York, a little pocket of Queens that is best remembered as the home of Rosie—the queen of Corona—in Paul Simon's song "Me and Julio Down By the Schoolyard."

I don't think there were many Julios in the neighborhood then, but there were plenty of Angelos, Tonys, Vinnies, Brunos, a couple of Nunzios, and yes, a full complement of Rosies. It was an Italian neighborhood, but more than that it was *our family street* in an Italian neighborhood. My grandfather, my dad's dad, was a builder. He owned many of the multifamily houses on the street and most of the families in them were related to us. My brothers were literally surrounded by family—aunts, uncles, and cousins—up and down the street on either side.

We moved from this little enclave when I was only a year old, so I don't remember any of it. But I feel like I know it because I heard so much about it from my brothers, especially Jim, who loved growing up there.

I think Nick loved it too, but the "take your brother along" thing must have started to wear thin at some point. He took Jim everywhere. And, since they were surrounded by family and this was the fifties, good, conscientious parents like ours thought nothing of allowing their kids to wander around the block and roam the neighborhood, since inevitably wherever they went, there was family around to keep an eye on them. Much of this Corona childhood survived in the adult Jim, especially the sense of wonder, discovery, and curiosity that had to have come from the unfettered freedom he had to roam the neighborhood as a child.

Jim talked all his life about how exciting it was to visit our Aunt Marion when he was young because she would let him do all kinds of fun stuff. He remembered specifically that she let him try to re-create the latest experiments from the *Mr. Wizard* TV show in her apartment. He loved to retell the story of boiling eggs in vinegar, making them as hard as rubber balls, and then bouncing them off the walls. Great fun, but more so for him, no doubt, than for my aunt, who was left with an apartment reeking of boiling vinegar! One night he stayed over at her apartment, and in the morning she told him he could have anything he wanted for breakfast. He chose Nedick's orange soda, and *she gave it to him*. I think he may have been more excited about that than he was about winning the national championship.

According to Nick, this was a theme that ran throughout Jim's life:

> Jim had to—just *had* to—have fun in whatever he did. He had a tremendous desire to make other people laugh, and to make himself laugh, and that was rooted in his childhood. The nuns at St. Leo's school used to take him from classroom to classroom when he was in first grade, and he'd do Jimmy Durante impersonations: "Driver, does this bus go over the George Washington bridge? 'Cause if it don't, we're gonna get awful wet. *Ka-cha, ka-cha.* Good night, Mrs. Calabash, wherever you are." When he came into my class, I'd sink down in my chair, humiliated. My friends would say, "Hey, isn't that your little brother?" and I'd claim I didn't know him.

"Take your brother along" also meant taking him to neighborhood games, and the unspoken addendum was, "and make sure he gets a chance to play." Since Nick and his friends were all four years older than him, Jim was introduced to rough and tumble competition at an early age. He believed he really was competing with the older kids, and tried very hard to keep up. One day he came home and proudly announced that he had hit a home run. My dad, thinking Nick and his friends had charitably misplayed a ball and let Jim run around the bases, took Nick aside to tell him that wasn't the best way to help Jim get better and learn to really compete. "Hey, we didn't do anything like that," Nick said. "He hit the ball over the fence." Jim was always the smallest, but he soon learned that somehow, some way, he could figure out how to hold his own with the big guys. Another seed had been planted.

"Take your brother along" also meant, amazingly to me, that they were allowed to go to Yankee Stadium, in the Bronx, *alone!* No adults! Nick was 13, Jimmy 9, and they rode the subway all the way to the Bronx and back by themselves. To this day, I can't believe my mother, who was so protective with me, let them do that. Not only did she let them go to the games, she'd pack them 15 or so meatball sandwiches to eat on the way there and during the game. It was a long day, Nick remembers:

> We'd get there about three hours before game time, to see the Yankees take batting practice. If you got there early, you could go into the right-field lower deck and try to catch a ball. One day Jimmy and I were out there and a batting practice home run came right at us. We jumped but it was just a little out of our reach. We turned around and saw it shatter the back of a wooden chair in the row behind us. Jimmy turned to me and said, "We're trying to catch *that?*"

It was a different era, obviously, with two kids riding subways all over the city by themselves, but some things never change, and one of the immutable rites of passage is that little kids get teased. A lot. Said Nick:

> Jimmy used to cry at the drop of a hat. In fact, when I'd finally had enough of "take your brother along," I'd turn to Fat Antny [that would be Anthony Joya, universally known on the streets of Corona as Fat Antny or Fat Joya] and say, "Hey Fat, which would you rather have, a million dollars or Jimmy's nose filled with pennies?" Jimmy would start bawling immediately and run home, which is what I wanted. Of course, then I'd get home and get a beating.

Of course, in fairness it must be said that Jim too sometimes wound up on the receiving end of a little hide tanning. This was no Dick and Tommy Smothers "mom-liked-you-best" routine. Our dad was a loving man devoted to his family, but he was strict—make no mistake about that— and clearly impartial when it came to calling a foul on his sons. Usually, like those times in a game when the ref calls one against your team and you know you've got no legitimate gripe, his discipline was fair whether it was directed at Nick, Jim, or myself.

Nick again:

> One Christmas Jimmy and I got a great set of Lionel trains. This was a real deluxe set, with different cars, tracks, scenery, buildings, everything. I was probably eight or nine at the time. Dad was having difficulty putting this complicated set together, and had spent hours and hours on it, getting increasingly frustrated. We all know the three scariest words at Christmas are "some assembly required," and I know I'm not the only kid who had learned to stay out of his dad's way at those times. Well, he was having a terrible time and was starting to lose his temper. All of a sudden, in marches five-year-old Jimmy, who looks at my exasperated father surrounded by all these parts and says, "Hey, don't cry on my shoulder." I was laughing so hard I had to put a towel in my mouth in the next room so my dad couldn't hear me. If he had, I know I'd have gotten spanked just like Jimmy did.

There are two things from these little childhood episodes that carried over into Jim's adult life, and I believe added to the apparent contradictions that seemed to be a part of his personality. First, and perhaps less significant, was a lifelong appreciation for good-natured teasing. I know this because I bore the brunt of it my whole life. But he liked to tease anybody and everybody, as long as it was in the spirit of fun. Nick says that he was good at it when he teased Jim, but Jim elevated it to an art form when he in turn teased me.

When I was about five years old, which meant Jim would have been about sixteen, he would often come home from school and play with me. We'd go to the backyard of our home on Long Island and play basketball on a little hoop my dad had built just for me. Jim would say, "Let's play to 100 and I'll spot you 90." Then he'd allow me to score the first seven or eight points, so I'd be ahead 98–0, really believing I was going to win. Of course, I don't even need to tell you what happened next. Not only would I lose 100–98, but Jim would start announcing the game and making crowd noises:

Valvano drives the baseline and *scores!* There's 10,000 people on their feet screaming and cheering on this incredible comeback! The other 100 people here in the arena . . . free tickets. Unfortunately, there's nobody in the crowd cheering for poor little Bobby.

Of course I'd run into the house crying for my mommy, who wouldn't even look up from her ironing. "Then don't play with him anymore," was all the comfort I got from her. Not play with Jimmy? What was she thinking about?

And so, like Charlie Brown believing that this time he really *was* going to kick the football, I'd be back the next day, repeating the process, perhaps in baseball, or backyard golf, or some other game that would inevitably end with Jim calling after me as I ran crying into the house: "Remember, you have never beaten me in *anything*. Ever!"

I don't think this had any long-term effect on me, other than the inability to blink my eyes in unison until I was 14.

The second part of this Corona childhood that carried over, and which is a more significant part of understanding Jim, is his sensitivity. He worked hard to hide it (and there's no shortage of people who would say he was successful!), but despite his sometimes coarse language and aggressive behavior, he never forgot the little boy—and Jim was always small even for his age, let alone playing with older kids—who was constantly hurt and teased. It gave him a connection with those people who were the underdogs, or who at least felt they were. It was a large part of who Jim was, and a large part of how he was able to pass the gift of believing in others on. You have to first really connect with someone before you can inspire them, move them, and motivate them, and Jim had that unique ability to relate to "the little guy," since he felt like he was one of them. He never had any desire to take Queens and Corona out of his life, and it stayed with him forever.

Another part of that childhood stayed with him too, and that was the competitiveness. He would use that to carve a place for himself in the next chapter of his life, the venue of which was the untamed wilderness of Long Island.

4

SEAFORD

EVERY FAMILY HAS ITS FAVORITE STORIES, AND OURS IS NO EXCEPTION. One of the classics in our family concerns how my brother Nick found out he had a new baby brother (me). He was playing in a junior varsity basketball game for Holy Cross High School in Queens in January of 1957. My dad, a basketball coach whose whole life revolved around athletics and his family, had managed to get away from his job and, after visiting my mom in the hospital, had hurried to the game. At halftime he came down to the Holy Cross bench and motioned to Nick.

"Nick, Nick!" he said excitedly. "Listen. I think you can take your guy baseline! Oh, and by the way," he added as an afterthought, "your mother had a baby boy." That was Rocco through and through, and it could just as easily have been Jimmy, he had so much of our dad in him.

Shortly after that incident our family found themselves in Seaford, Long Island, having moved from Queens when my dad was given the opportunity to create the athletic program for a brand-new high school being built on land that had been an old potato farm. Rocky Valvano, who had coached and taught for his whole life in the parochial school system in New York City, would now be breaking new ground in the wilderness of Long Island.

My father had been a terrific athlete. He didn't talk much about it, but I later found meticulously kept scrapbooks that detailed his playing career, primarily in basketball and baseball, although I don't think there was a sport he didn't try somewhere along the way. He played on many semipro teams, including teams in the New York–Penn pro basketball league, and briefly with teams in the Basketball Association of America, which was the forerunner of the NBA. He also spent a brief time in the

Yankees organization's minor league system. Much of this was done while holding other jobs, including teaching and coaching. He would even referee often, ultimately assuming the role of rules interpreter for all of Nassau County.

I've often said that the greatest endorsement my dad gave his sons for the value of sports was simply his own love for them. He never pushed us to play anything, but this was a man who loved his life, and his life was filled with sports. You know how some people say "TGIF"—thank God it's Friday? With Pop it was always "TGIM"—thank God it's Monday. He loved teaching and coaching and the young people involved in both.

Here was a guy who at some stages of his life was doing *all* of the following at one time: teaching, coaching, officiating, running a gym for the Police Athletic League, and, oh yeah, playing semipro basketball and baseball. He would often play two games for two different teams on the same day, one under an assumed name. I found this out by accident while looking through his scrapbooks. The box score for a particular game didn't include his name and I asked him why the clipping was in the book. "Oh, I was Bill Costello for that game," he said. A certain Rocky Rabinowitz also had a pretty good game for the House of David, an all-Jewish team.

He loved to play, and he loved to tell stories about the games he played in. Do you know why basketball players are called *cagers*? My dad did. There were some playing facilities that were surrounded with netting, like the glass that surrounds hockey rinks, only much higher, creating in effect a cage. There were varying rules regarding the cage: some places allowed the ball to be passed off the netting and yet remain in play. That's where the term *cagers* came from. There were even courts in basements with support beams *in the court of play*, and some teams would run plays using the support beam as a pick, just like the goal posts in the NFL were used as an extra defensive lineman 30 years ago.

Believe it or not, in the early days of the pro basketball league they had to use two hands to dribble the ball. When my dad was about to make the leap to play in that league he spent the whole summer beforehand practicing his two-handed dribble. He got pretty good at it, and then a month before the season started they changed the rule to make it consistent with all the amateur leagues.

I personally can't imagine the game in such a formative stage. Some leagues played quarters, some played halves like colleges do, and some even played "thirds," like hockey! Talk about pioneers! The game wasn't the same from league to league, or even from year to year in the same league. To be a small part of that had to be great fun, and very exciting. The people, the places, the sights, sounds, and smells, the offbeat and eclectic—my dad loved it all, and all this rubbed off on Jim and infused in him a lifelong love and enthusiasm for the game.

At Seaford High School, my dad brought home all the white canvas basketball shoes his students wore and dyed them kelly green—the Seaford colors—in our bathtub. The house would stink for days from that dye! But he did it. He also painted the alternate panels of a practice basketball green and white, and I thought that was just about the coolest thing I had ever seen. (I was a pretty sophisticated five-year-old at the time.)

Much as he loved his job and any kind of athletic competition (coaching, playing, or just watching), it was clear that with Dad, family always came first. Let's go back to Queens and listen to a story I heard Jim tell many times over the years:

> When I was growing up in Corona, we used to play every game you could think of on the streets—stickball mainly, but also baseball, tackle football (yes, tackle!), roller hockey, you name it. And of course, occasionally accidents would happen.
>
> One day we were playing baseball and one of the kids hit a ball that broke a neighbor's window. We promised him we'd pay for it, but he was mad and made us quit playing. We begged and pleaded, but that was it; he kicked us off the street and made us go home. When my dad got home, he saw a bunch of long-faced kids moping around and asked why we weren't out playing ball as usual.
>
> When we told him, it was his turn to get mad. "He must be ridiculous," he said. That was an expression he used all the time, and one that family members still smile about when they think of him. "He must be ridiculous. It's not his street, it's everybody's street. We'll pay for his window, he knows that. You kids want to play? Get out there in the street and play."
>
> We charged back out on the street and Dad confronted the irate neighbor. "Whatsa matter with you Tony? Who says these kids can't play? We'll pay for your window. They wanna play, they're gonna play."

We started getting a little cocky now that "Big Rock" was
on our side. We started *aiming* for that neighbor's windows,
and calling our shots like a pool player. "Next pitch, third floor,
second window on the right . . ."

Well, maybe that last part was a little exaggeration, but that was Jim. He
loved a good story and saw nothing wrong with making a good story a little bit better. The point is that for Rocky, and later for Jim, family came first.

My dad was almost killed in a car accident while traveling in the New
York–Penn League. He was in the back seat when the car skidded on ice
near Utica, New York, and slid underneath a disabled tractor trailer, shear-
ing off the top of the vehicle and killing his two teammates in the front
seat. He was in a coma for a while, and he remembered waking up with
tubes and wires running everywhere in and out of his body. His face was
smashed and even when he recovered it took a long time before his fea-
tures returned to normal.

Dad loved a good surprise, so he didn't tell anyone on the day he was
released from the hospital. He just took a cab home, and when the family
opened the door, there he was. The shock was all the more severe because
he was wearing a hat, which he absolutely *never* did, to hide the disfigure-
ment of his face and head. This all happened years before I was born, of
course, and his recovery was so complete that he was regarded as a good-
looking man until the day he died in 1985. In fact, I probably never would
have known about the accident if I hadn't read about it and asked him. He
had no physical scars and, other than the fact that he would never sleep in
a car when someone else was driving (or when he himself was, for that
matter!), there were no lasting effects.

Except, perhaps, one. I think the accident made it easier for Dad to
keep the relative importance of winning and losing in perspective. For
him, the game—the *playing*—was everything, and this became true for
Jim as well. For all their competitiveness, they both had this as an anchor,
a base, a means to keep themselves grounded.

At Seaford my dad ran the phys. ed. department and the athletic
department and coached basketball. Harry Curtis was the football and
baseball coach, and since Jim was a three-sport athlete, these two coaches
had a huge influence on his life and development. Technically, he played
football for three years, but he didn't play much as a sophomore and was
hurt as a junior before he made All-County at quarterback his senior year.

Baseball, however, was probably his best sport. He led the varsity in hitting as a freshman, became All–Long Island at shortstop his senior year, and even got a look from the Kansas City Athletics, who wanted to sign him.

During his four years in high school, Jim played for only two coaches—my dad and Harry Curtis. Fortunately, their mutual respect and similar coaching philosophies ensured that Jim got consistent messages from each. Both were considered disciplinarians, but both believed they could give their teams a system that was structured yet also instilled a love of the game and permitted individual development. When he was in his midthirties, Jim could recall every football game he played in from the eighth grade on—where the game was played, team, score, key plays, everything. It was astounding. If he could recall that in such detail, I'm sure he had little trouble remembering points that were hammered home day after day for over three years by two coaches whom he loved, one of whom he lived with.

One of my father's key tenets as a coach was that his players needed him more after a loss than they did after a win. He believed that when you lost, the most important thing you could do was figure out what the game had taught you that could make you better. Like many good coaches, he'd schedule games against tougher opponents early in the season so his kids could learn to deal with adversity and use the losses to improve their game. I was reminded of that years later when people talked about Jim's ability to use the regular season to "tinker" with his team so they were playing their best in March.

Curtis tells a great story of how both those principles—learning from adversity and "being there" for your kids when you lose—came together during Jim's senior year football season:

> We were trailing a nearby rival, MacArthur High School, 14–12 late in the game, but driving deep in their territory. On a third-down play, Jim got shaken up and play was stopped. He was OK, but the rules at that time said that if play was stopped, the player had to come out for at least one play. So here we were, fourth-and-inches, key play of the game, with my quarterback on the sidelines. We only had about 12 kids who played much, so I had to move John Hoverman from end to quarterback for one play. I sent in a kid off the bench and told him to just stand in the end position, not to move, and sent the play in with him, which was a quarterback sneak. I figure if we can't gain six

inches and the first down, we don't deserve to win. So anyway, this kid scrambles the instructions, and Hoverman takes the snap, starts rolling out, and gets tackled behind the line of scrimmage. Ball game. MacArthur takes over on downs, runs out the clock, and we lose.

At the next practice, all we did was practice running plays in from the bench. I'd give a kid a play at one end of the field and he had to sprint 120 yards to the other end and repeat the play to a teammate who had to sprint back and give it to me. Not a lot of laughs at this practice. After we had done this a while, the point had clearly been made, and practice was over. The players were on one knee listening to my comments when I paused for a moment, took off my hat, and a bird that happened by chose that moment to . . . well, you can guess what he did on my head.

There wasn't a sound. Just a stone cold silence. I reached up, wiped the dripping mess from my head, and said, "It's OK . . . you can go ahead and laugh." And laugh they did, led by No. 11, rolling around on the ground he was laughing so hard. We didn't lose another game that year and wound up 8–2.

Despite the fact that his two coaches were stern disciplinarians (and one also happened to be his father *and* the athletic director), Jim never lacked the courage to have a little fun, and to stand up to his coach.

Another story that's part of the family lore also dates back to Jim's football days at Seaford High. Their arch rival was Wantagh, the next town over, and it was always the biggest game of the year. In the Seaford-Wantagh game of Jim's senior year, Seaford was leading by a single point late in the game with the ball just inside Wantagh territory. Coach Curtis called all the plays and certainly could be expected to make the call in the situation Seaford now faced, a fourth-and-inches with just under two minutes to go. Wantagh was out of timeouts, so there was no doubt a punt was called for in order to pin them deep. Curtis clearly signaled with his leg that that was indeed what he wanted Jim to do, but in the huddle Jim said, "The hell with kicking it; we're going to get the six inches, keep the ball, and the game is over." He turned to his fullback, Billy Freese, and said, "You better make the first down because if you don't, you won't have to worry about coach kicking your ass. I'll kill you first."

Seaford did, in fact, make that first down. The game should have been over after a few more plays but instead, Curtis called timeout and after giving Jim a solid (but affectionate) *boink* on the helmet, reamed him out good on the sidelines in front of the bench before letting him go back in and run out the clock.

That night *Newsday*, the Long Island newspaper, called my dad to get some quotes about the game because they hadn't been able to reach Coach Curtis. Jim, home alone at the time, answered the phone and, finding out who it was and what they wanted, told them to hang on a minute. Coming back and lowering his voice an octave, he said, "Yeah, this is Rocky. Go ahead."

Well, the next day's paper featured a story about the great win and how proud the athletic director was of the team. It mentioned that he was especially proud of Jim Valvano's play and his courage in going for the crucial first down late in the game. On Monday morning Harry Curtis made a beeline for Rocky's office, demanding to know why he had made those public comments, and of course my dad, who hadn't even seen the paper, didn't know what he was talking about. It took them about 30 seconds to sort out what had happened; they promptly summoned Jim to the office. Jim, who had been sweating it out all weekend, did the best he could: "Well, it *was* a big win . . . and everyone would have been disappointed if there was no story. Since you two weren't available . . ."

It may as well have been Peoria, because it didn't play any better in Seaford than it would have there. Jim would gladly have settled for another affectionate *boink* on the helmet instead of the lecture he got. Fortunately or unfortunately, he didn't have too many privileges that could be taken away. (Neither he nor Nick were allowed to get their driver's license until they graduated . . . *from college!*) Nevertheless, Jim got two things he loved out of the experience—attention and a good laugh.

Out on Long Island, the world was opening up around Jim. He was meeting people from other ethnic backgrounds who introduced him to cultural experiences that were different from anything he had known growing up in our close-knit, Italian neighborhood in Queens. He couldn't believe the foods some of these families ate: no lasagna or prosciutto, no tomato gravy sandwiches. And there were no more Brunos or Nunzios, and only a few "Antnys," only now they were "Anthony." And the other names! Jim used to like to say that the first kid he met was named "Rusty." Rusty? Jimmy thought he had a condition.

He also met Pamela Susan Levine—the first girl he met, as he said, who didn't have a mustache. He thought her name was Levini and that she was Italian, and for her part, she took one look at his nose and thought he was Jewish. At any rate, they became friends, soon more than friends. Of all the things Jim took from Seaford, though he didn't know it at the time, one was ultimately to be the beginning of his new family. For he had met his future wife.

Much as he liked playing with his five-year-old brother, Jim didn't like babysitting me, which he had to do from time to time. One night, rather than stay home he had us walk the mile or so to Pam's house. It was a cool fall night. Pam's family had guests so we were in the backyard. I was running around trying to amuse myself while they played kissy face, and it wasn't too long before I had to go to the bathroom. "Just wait a minute," Jim said. "We're leaving soon." Another 10 minutes passed. "Jimmy, I really have to go bad," I told him. Same response: "Hold it in," he said. "We're going to be going home in just a minute." This went on for another half hour or so, until it was too late. Even at five years old I could feel the embarrassment of my "accident," but it was nothing compared to the shame and humiliation Jim felt leading me into his girlfriend's house during a social gathering with his wet-all-over little brother in tow.

My five-year-old mind made a quick calculation and determined it was all my fault. Jim seemed to agree, because all the way home he'd let me get about five feet ahead of him and then, mumbling under his breath, come up and kick me hard in the butt. Grumble, walk, kick . . . grumble, walk, kick. A mile of this. Until I was 11, every time I saw somebody kiss I had to run to the john.

There was a serious side to this too, though. One of the reasons Jim was reluctant to ask if I could go into the house was because he wasn't welcome there. The Levines didn't want their daughter seeing a non-Jewish boy. When Jim would ring their bell, Pam's parents would answer the door and yell up the stairs, "It's him." Jim would say, "It's *Jim*, not *him*. Hard *J* sound." After many years, three wonderful daughters, and a warm relationship with Pam's family, it became easy to joke about it; but at the time it hurt Jim. It also made him sensitive to anyone who had trouble finding acceptance because of race, religion, or ancestry.

He was also sympathetic if any of his kids had to play under any unusual scrutiny. He learned to feel this way because of the issue of nepotism, which he became aware of as early as his sophomore year in high school. My dad had been so conscious of it that he didn't even let our older brother, Nick, start on the basketball team until his junior year, when it became so obvious that he was one of the best players on the team that Dad couldn't avoid it. I mentioned earlier that Jim started as a freshman on the varsity baseball team, and one day my dad wanted to make sure it wasn't because of who his father was. "C'mon, Rock," Harry Curtis told him, "you know me a lot better than that. He's playing because he deserves to play."

But Jim always felt the scrutiny. In his sophomore year there was an article in *Newsday* titled "Coach's Son Won't Shoot," which chronicled the story of how my dad had to bench Jimmy because he wouldn't shoot. As the coach's son and a sophomore, it made Jim very uncomfortable to come in and take shots away from upperclassmen. But he was passing up shots on plays where he was the primary option, and the coach, father or no father, had to bench him to get the point across.

Of course when the spotlight was on, that was a different story. Back in the sixties, WPIX-TV in New York would do the High School Game of the Week. On TV! Keep in mind, this was before the mind-numbingly large amount of televised sports we now have at *every* level. This was a high school game! On the tube! With Marty Glickman—the legendary Marty Glickman, former voice of the New York Knicks and New York Giants—calling the game. In what should have been an omen, little Jimmy hit three straight jumpers from the corner against the best team in their division. I wish there were an AP poll available to see where this ultimately ranked in his mind with the National Championship and the breakfast at Aunt Marion's after the vinegar-boiled eggs. It would have been up there, trust me. Jim was not shy in talking about his exploits, and any number of his friends from all walks of life can tell the story of the three jumpers from the corner against Malverne, or his five-for-five day at the plate against New Hyde Park.

Seaford was a wonderful place for all of us to grow up, and, aided by the nostalgic glow of a selective memory, it seems a magical time. The green and white colors, the *Vikings* nickname chosen by my dad and Harry Curtis, the logo painted in the gym: for us, these were the "pioneering" days of our athletic development. And the way my dad labored over the details of every aspect of his athletic program became a permanent part of Jim's character and development. He seemed to take as much interest in designing new stationery as the head coach at Johns Hopkins as he did in the most sought-after recruit. His enthusiasm for every part of the program was rooted in his Seaford experience and in watching our dad.

But when it came time for Jim to pick a college, despite the fact that he was an all-star on three winning teams in three sports, the recruiters were not exactly lined up. Back then recruiting was nowhere near as sophisticated as it is today, and despite the fact that the Kansas City A's had a real interest in him, no one really offered him a scholarship.

He had narrowed his choices to three schools (two of which are Division III today, although that classification wasn't in place yet at the time): Albright College in Pennsylvania, Colby College in Maine, and Rutgers University, which, despite being my dad's alma mater, offered Jim only the opportunity to walk on to play basketball or baseball.

New Brunswick, New Jersey, would become the scene for the next chapter of Jim's life and, like leaving Queens for the suburbs of Long Island, this too would be an education and an adventure.

5

RUTGERS

RUTGERS. THE STATE UNIVERSITY OF NEW JERSEY. BIRTHPLACE OF college football in 1869. Alma mater of Milton Friedman, one of the nation's great economists; Ozzie Nelson, band leader and sweater-wearing TV star of the fifties; and poet Joyce Kilmer, among others. All three are members of the Hall of Distinguished Alumni at the university.

According to his own testimony, Rutgers is also the alma mater of the cartoon character Mr. Magoo. When Jim Valvano enrolled in the fall of 1963, his chances of someday being selected for the Hall of Distinguished Alumni were about the same as that famous cartoon character's. He wasn't there on a basketball scholarship, and in fact it was by no means certain that he would even be on the basketball team. Most athletes find out quickly that all the success and honors they earned in high school mean little or nothing at the college level, and Jim was no exception. It was a whole new ballgame.

College basketball itself was a different ballgame in the midsixties. Rutgers didn't play in a big arena like they do today. Their home games were in the Physical Education Center, where the team benches were up against a portable wall, on the other side of which was the swimming pool. Even the luxury boxes were . . . wait a minute, there were no luxury boxes. There wasn't much of a winning tradition, either. During Jim's freshman year the varsity was 5–17, but that turned out to be the only losing season under new coach Bill Foster. In his eight seasons at the helm he brought the Scarlet Knights into national prominence with record-setting win totals, games at Madison Square Garden, and a trip to the National Invitational Tournament (NIT). That tournament, once the biggest and best in the country, had lost some of its luster by then, but was still nearly equal to the NCAA in prestige. Bill Foster brought a new excitement to Rutgers basketball in the sixties.

Bob Lloyd became Rutgers' first basketball All-American in 1967, scoring over 2,000 points in an era when eligibility was restricted to three years. He never averaged less than 25 points per game in his three varsity seasons, and led the nation in free throw percentage. He and a walk-on named Jim Valvano formed one of the nation's best backcourts their senior year, scoring 1,335 points between them and leading Rutgers to its first ever NIT berth. Here's how Lloyd remembers first meeting Jim:

> I was getting settled in my room and Jim lived just across the hall. He saw me putting my shoes away and asked, "What are those?" "They're shoe trees," I answered. "Shoe trees? What do they do?" "You put them in the shoes and they keep them stretched out, so the soles don't wear out." Jim stared at me with a blank look on his face. "Why don't you just get new shoes?" he asked. This was the first time I had ever met the guy, and I didn't know what to think.
>
> A little later we decided to go out and get something to eat, and when we came to an intersection, Jim said, "Quick. Take my hand." "Take your hand, what are you, kidding? What for?" "Just take it," Jim said, grabbing my hand and arm. We walked into the intersection, and he started to do a clumsy, spastic walk, hanging on to me so I couldn't get loose. Cars started slamming on their brakes and fishtailing on all sides of us, with him making it look like I was dragging this poor helpless creature into the middle of traffic. Traffic was stopping and I was getting dirty looks from all the drivers while Jim, as soon as we got to the other side, straightened up and walked away like nothing had happened. I stood there, dumbfounded, with the drivers yelling at me. I thought to myself, "This guy is crazy . . ."

I'm convinced one of his great ambitions through all the years I knew him was to embarrass me. He would go to any length, and often showed great ingenuity. After games, we'd often go to a diner called the Town House to get something to eat. It was a popular hangout for Rutgers people, so there was always somebody waving, saying hello, or stopping by our table. Jim would say, "Would you be embarrassed if I did 'the pimple' right here?" This happened to be his favorite way to disgust and embarass me, so he knew my answer. "Of course I would. Don't even *think* about it." Of course, that's all he needed to hear, so he'd order a dish of vanilla ice cream, put the whole scoop in his mouth, and as soon as he was sure he had an audience, squeeze his cheeks and squirt it all back into the bowl. "Look, Bob, I'm a pimple!" he'd say. "I know, Jim, I know. I've seen it. That's very nice . . . "

Of course this gag had its desired effect on Bob because he was, and still is, a very proper and neat person, which made him, in Jim's mind, the perfect target. "Jim would start in on me," Bob said, "and I'd think, 'Uh, oh, here we go again, I'm about to become the abusee.' And sure enough, I'd be the brunt of a joke or story. Often they were stories all of us had heard before, but regardless, we couldn't help it, and soon we'd be laughing so hard our sides would hurt."

Jim's barbs could occur on the court as well as off. Said Lloyd:

Once we were tied late in the game and I got fouled, with about two seconds left. Now this was back when you'd shoot one-shot fouls rather than get the ball out of bounds. I was leading the nation in free throw percentage at the time, but I went to the line and missed, sending the game into overtime. Late in the overtime, I got fouled again, this time in a one-and-one situation, but this time we were down by one point, again with about two seconds left. I got to the line, and honestly, I was very nervous. It was like golf, right after you miss a little two footer, you're a little jittery next time facing the same putt. Just before the referee handed me the ball Jim came up, whispered something in my ear, and slapped me on the behind. Fortunately for us, I made the free throws and we won by one point. After the game was over, a reporter approached me and asked me about the free throws. "I saw your roommate come over and give you a little pat on the back. Was he encouraging you after your earlier miss?" "Not exactly," I said. "Jim leaned over and whispered in my ear, 'You got us into this mess, you get us out.'"

Bob Lloyd loves recounting these stories, but he's quick to add that Jim was a pretty good basketball player in his own right, calling him the best defensive player he ever played against, and crediting his own scoring ability to the fact that Jim defended him almost every day in practice.

Mike Krzyzewski agrees. He played at Army when Jim was at Rutgers and thinks Jim never got the recognition he deserved. "Bob Lloyd was a terrific player, and because of that Jimmy got overlooked sometimes. Plus, the college game wasn't covered like it is now with all the TV and radio, so it was easier to be overlooked then. With everything he accomplished later in his life, that became another reason to forget that he really was a very fine college player."

Said Lloyd:

> Even though I wondered about the guy's sanity when I first met him, my other immediate reaction was that this guy was pretty bright. He liked to clown around, but it didn't take long to see that he was interested in a lot of different things, and was just a very smart guy.
>
> He was tremendously competitive in everything. Basketball certainly, but pinball, cards, miniature golf, you name it. I remember one time we played that game where you try to get the little paper "football" to hang over the edge of the table for a touchdown. We got so mad over that we didn't speak to each other for a week.
>
> Jim always believed that he was going to win. Always. Once Sunoco started a promotion where you could get game pieces to try to win money every time you pulled into their gas station. No purchase necessary. Jim spent an entire Saturday driving to every Sunoco in New Jersey getting game pieces. Other times he'd buy just two gallons of gas at six different stations, rather than fill up at one, in order to get more game pieces. We had them all over our apartment for about a month.

He liked to play the class clown, and often told the story of his freshman biology lab. He and his lab partner, Joe DiCenza, were not exactly Einsteins when it came to science, and knew better than to raise their hands to try to contribute to the discussion in class. On one particular day they were about to begin the dissection of a frog. The procedure was called the "double pithing of a frog." As a means to start the lesson, the professor asked, "What exactly is a double pithing of a frog?" Jim's hand shot up, and the professor, surprised and pleased, said, "Yes, Mr. Valvano?" "That's where I pith on the frog, and then Joey pithes on it too."

Said Bob Lloyd:

> After our sophomore year, Jim and I were working Coach Foster's basketball camp, and after the session one day he called Jim in to have a talk with him. When Jimmy came out he was furious. "Foster thinks I'm getting by just on ability alone and that I'm not working hard enough at it," Jimmy fumed. "I can't believe he'd say that. I kill myself in practice." And it's true, he did; but coach was talking about the off-season, the summer, the additional work you have to do year round to get better. Jimmy had always played three different sports—he was still playing baseball as a freshman at Rutgers—and I think this was the first time he started to look at basketball as a year-round commitment to get better. He clearly started to work very hard that summer, and we'd push each other, playing a lot of one-on-one as well as battling in practice. But make no mistake, he never lost the clown in him.
>
> During our senior year, when we made it to the semifinals of the NIT, there were about 19,000 people in Madison Square Garden as we were getting ready to play Walt Frazier's Southern Illinois team. Before the game, Bill Foster gave us a great speech about how no one expected us to get this far, how good the year had been, and how we should just go out there and relax. Play our game. Have some fun out there. It was a good speech, and just as we're in the final huddle ready to head out onto the court, Coach Foster said, "Let's just be loosey-goosey out there." Jim looked over at me and said, "Bob, you be loosey-goosey. I'll be ducky-wucky."

That NIT season was special indeed. I was 10 years old at the time, and I remember so much of it. The cheerleaders were all men (Rutgers was all male at the time) and they were great gymnasts, doing entertaining and funny routines during the timeouts. The one that got the crowd most excited was when they simply formed the letters *N*, *I*, and *T* while lying in formation on the court. The fans would go crazy. It's hard to explain to people who weren't around then what a big deal the NIT was. There were only 23 teams who received NCAA bids at that time, and the NIT invited only 14 teams. Thirty-seven teams in the entire country in the postseason! Plus, the entire NIT was played at Madison Square Garden, not just the Final Four, as is now the case. So it really was a big deal.

For a 10-year-old kid, it was pure magic. Because of my big brother, I got to meet New York Knicks stars Cazzie Russell and Dick Van Arsdale and Celtics coach Red Auerbach. I got comedian Soupy Sales' autograph (he was *huge*) as he watched his beloved Marshall Thundering Herd in action. I went down to the Rangers' dressing room, used by the Rutgers team, and put on Hall of Famer Eddie Giacomin's goalie glove! At 10 years old! It felt like it was going to break my arm off, but hey, he had to catch Bobby Hull's slap shot with that thing. I remember being struck by the fact that there were only two showers. Our high school had more than that. No wonder they built a new Garden the next year.

But the most memorable meeting was also the most frightening. Muhammad Ali, or Cassius Clay as he was sometimes still called, was training at the Garden for a title defense against Zora Folley. Like the Rutgers team, he was staying in the hotel just across the street from the Garden. After one of the games, my parents, Jim, and I were eating in the coffee shop in the lobby of the hotel. Right in the middle of the meal who should come walking through but the champ himself! All alone, no entourage, no hangers-on, no bodyguards. I jumped up to try to get his autograph, but he was gone before I could get to him. This was at the height of the debate about his name change, and the papers were full of stories about him. I remembered reading that he had taunted Ernie Terrell for the better part of 12 rounds, refusing to knock him out and screaming "What's my name? What's my name?" at him for much of the fight.

My mother knew how much I wanted his autograph and she was determined to help me get it. She was seated closest to the door he had exited through, and when it suddenly opened and he reappeared, she yelled out at the top of her voice, "Oh, Cassius!" You could have heard a pin drop. Maybe you remember that old E. F. Hutton commercial, where the businessman says, "Well, my broker is E. F. Hutton, and E. F. Hutton says. . . ." At that point there's dead silence as everyone in the room leans over to hear the sage advice. That's how quiet it was in this New York coffee shop when my mom had the temerity to shout out the forbidden name. Everybody, and I do mean *everybody*—waiters, waitresses, people eating, people leaving, busboys—absolutely froze. They stopped chewing. They stopped talking. They stopped drinking. They stopped with forks lifted halfway to their mouths. And they all stared at our table.

Slowly, Ali made his way toward our table, glowering. I had visions of the next day's headlines: "Rangers Beat Wings; Knicks Fall; Raging Muslim Kills Italian Family." I was 10 years old; what did I know? I swear my heart has never beaten faster. I could actually hear it. As Ali approached our table, my mother gulped and said, "Oh, I am so sorry. I should have said *Muhammad*." With that, the champ flashed his million-dollar smile, signed his autograph for me, and went on his way. I've loved him ever since, especially since he didn't punch my mother.

He could have punched Jim, though. After the first-round game, Jimmy ran into Ali's trainer, Angelo Dundee, in the hotel lobby. "Hey, *paisano*, nice game the other night," Dundee said. Jimmy, never at a loss for words, said, "Thanks, Mr. Dundee. Hey, I know Ali is training downstairs at the Garden. Any chance I might be able to get into the ring with him and spar a little?" Dundee was happy to play along. "Sure," he said, "come on down tomorrow morning and I'll get you in for a round or two."

Well, the next day, with a break in their practice, a few of the Rutgers players made their way downstairs. All of a sudden, Ali stopped his workout and turned to the crowd. "Where's that basketball player who thinks he can whup the champ?" he asked, and all eyes turned to the Rutgers players, who looked straight at Jim. "Let's get him into the ring and see what he can do."

At that point Jim thought the joke had gone far enough, thank you very much, and tried to slink away. But his teammates thought otherwise, attempting to pick him up and carry him into the ring. Meanwhile, Ali played to the hysterical crowd. "Look at him! He's so scared you couldn't melt him and *pour* him into the ring! You see this little finger? I'll knock him out with this one little finger." Knowing discretion to be the better part of valor, Jim finally managed to escape through his teammates' defenses.

Later, Dundee cornered Jim. "Jimmy, what'd you run for? I had it all worked out—we had photographers from *Newsday*, *Time*, *Newsweek*, the *Daily News*, everybody who was here wanted that picture. He wasn't gonna hurt you. You would have been in every magazine in the country!" This may have been the last time Jim ran from publicity, albeit unknowingly. As a little footnote to this story, I interviewed Angelo Dundee for my radio show in 1999 and, astonishingly, he recalled the story in every detail. It was funny to hear it again, and from a different source and perspective, and nice to verify its authenticity. I mean, if you can't trust Angelo Dundee, who can you trust?

Rutgers had made it to the NIT semifinals by beating Utah State 78–76 in the first round and New Mexico 65–60 in the second. This had already created some memorable moments as recalled by Bill Foster:

> We had just beaten Utah State in the first round for Rutgers' first NIT win ever. The bus returned to campus and we were greeted by fans and cheerleaders who were celebrating the win. As each player got off the bus, the crowd would cheer and the cheerleaders would give the players a kiss. I looked up and saw Jim getting off and heard the crowd cheer. Then I looked up and saw him climbing back in the window so he could come out again! Each time the crowd would cheer and the cheerleaders would kiss him again. He must have done that three or four times.

Rutgers now faced a very good Southern Illinois team led by Walt Frazier and Dick Garrett in the second game of the semifinal doubleheader at the sold-out Garden. The first game had seen Al McGuire's Marquette team dispose of Marshall 83–78. I couldn't leave early to go get a hot dog because it went right down to the wire. As soon as it was over I made a dash for the concession stand. The lines were already long and I knew I'd probably miss the introductions of the Rutgers players, and especially my favorite part, where the opponents were introduced and our fans looked up from their newspapers to yell, "Who's he?" after each one. But I really got concerned and irritated when I knew the game had started and heard huge cheers from the crowd while I waited helplessly in line. I hurried back to the main arena. There was a timeout on the court. As I walked down the aisle, I passed my cousin, who said, "Wasn't your brother unbelievable?" Then he walked away, probably headed for his own hot dog, before I could ask him what he meant. What had happened?

I got to my seat and saw that Rutgers was leading by nine points, and my dad said, "Jimmy just made eight shots in a row, missed one, then made another. He has 18 points already!"

My big brother, my hero, had just had the greatest moment in his entire athletic career in front of 19,000 screaming fans in Madison Square Garden and I was out getting a hot dog! I felt like I had let him down, and maybe even jinxed the team as SIU switched to a zone in the second half, clamped down on Jimmy and Bob Lloyd, and went on to win 79–70. The next day Rutgers would come back to beat Marshall in the consolation game, and both Bob and Jim were named to the all-tournament first team.

It was a heady time for Rutgers basketball, for Jim, and especially for Bob Lloyd, who was about to become Rutgers' first All-American. Fortunately, both Bob and Jim shared a self-deprecating sense of humor that enabled them to keep things in perspective. Said Lloyd:

> It seemed like whenever we got too cocky or too full of our-selves, something would happen to deflate our egos. Our first two years at Rutgers, the only "official" clothes we had were old-fashioned sweatshirts and sweatpants, certainly not any-thing to be proud to be seen in. But our junior year, Coach Foster got us all team blazers with the official university seal on the front breast pocket. These were sharp and we were really proud of them. Our senior year, Jim and I were walking toward the gym for a game, all decked out in our blazers, with our Rutgers gym bags, probably strutting and hoping to be noticed by as many people as possible. About two blocks from the gym a huge dog came bounding out of nowhere and started to chase us. For all our differences, Jim and I had one thing in common: we were both absolutely terrified of dogs. There was no place to go so we scrambled up onto the roof of a nearby parked car. There we were with our blazers and Rutgers gym bags, on top of the car, when some 14-year-old kids came by and recog-nized us. "Hey, don't you guys play for Rutgers?" they asked. We didn't feel too cool anymore.
>
> Another time, near the end of our senior year, Jimmy and I were supposed to be featured speakers at a CYO banquet. It was a pretty big deal, about 350 people, and the night before we were in the apartment and I was working hard on my speech. I asked him what he was going to talk about, and he said, "Ah, I'm just going to wing it. What about you?" I said, "You know that speech we heard Lefty Dreisell give where he

took the letters of the word *athlete* and talked about each one: *a* is for attitude, *t* is for teamwork, and so on? I think I'm going to do something along those lines." Well, the next night we were at the banquet and Jim was scheduled to speak first. He got up, thanked the monsignor, stared right at me, and wouldn't you know it, stole the idea, word for word. "The word *athlete* is made up of seven letters. *A* is for attitude . . ." I couldn't believe it. I had people come up to me afterward and say, "Why were you writing so frantically while Jimmy was talking? He gave a great speech. How come you weren't listening?"

After graduation, Lloyd signed a contract to play in the ABA and Jim was offered a spot on Bill Foster's coaching staff. But before Bob could go to the pros and Jim could begin his coaching career, there was the little matter of military service. The Vietnam War was raging and if the stakes hadn't been so high, the idea of Bob and Jim in some M.A.S.H.-like unit could have been the stuff of which sitcoms are made. Fortunately for our nation, perhaps, they were both put in the reserves and kept stateside.

After their tour was up life moved on for both. Bob played two years in the ABA for the Nets (setting a long-standing record for consecutive free throws) before going on to a successful business career, and Jim began his coaching career at his alma mater. Their lives took different paths, but over 20 years later, still friends, they were to be reunited again in much different circumstances.

6

COACH

THE COACHING PROFESSION IS LIKE MOST OTHERS IN THAT YOU START at the bottom, pay your dues, and work your way up. Before Jim entered the national spotlight with the high-profile job at North Carolina State, he had earned his stripes with stops as an assistant at Rutgers, head coach at Johns Hopkins, assistant at Connecticut, head coach at Bucknell, and head coach at Iona.

After Jim's senior year, Bill Foster decided to invite him to join his coaching staff. Said Foster:

> We were happy to add Jim to our staff. He had the interest, and the knowledge, and his personality was such that I felt he would greatly add to our staff at Rutgers.
>
> I always felt that Jim was a terrific "bench" coach, and could react to situations in a way that made him stand out from many of his associates. I saw this in him as soon as he started working for me, and felt he got better and better at it throughout his career.

It didn't take Jim long to discover that *working* for Bill Foster was going to be a lot different than *playing* for him. A great many basketball players who go into coaching give it up after a year or two for one simple reason: they expect coaching to be like playing. When Jim started as an assistant varsity coach and the freshman head coach at Rutgers, he began to see Bill Foster differently. Now he was no longer his "coach"; he was a successful professional from whom Jim could learn a great deal. And the first thing he learned was that coaching was *nothing* like playing, but that in fact he was going to enjoy it every bit as much.

Here's a story he told about another lesson he learned early:

> It was the first day of practice at Rutgers. This was really try-outs for guys who wanted to be walk-ons, so there were maybe 100 guys in the gym waiting for me. In what later became a pattern for me, I discovered that day that when I got excited about something, like a first practice or a game, it was accompanied by a call from nature.
>
> I was *really* excited that day—my first practice! My first team! So, with just minutes left until practice was scheduled to start, I hustled into the john. Unfortunately for me, and much to my chagrin, there was no paper. Anywhere! No toilet paper in my stall, or in any other stall. Absolutely none. Zero, zilch, nada. No paper towels. I mean nothing, and practice was ready to start any minute. I could hear shouts and balls bouncing in the gym and could imagine the players wondering, "Where the heck is coach?"
>
> Desperate times call for desperate measures. Let's just say my nice new "Rutgers Basketball" shirt died a hero. That problem solved, now I was late for practice *and* I had no shirt. I raced to the top of the stairs and opened the door. Standing there glaring at me with his hands on his hips was Coach Foster. The next day when I got to the office there was a note from him saying, "The first rule of coaching is always be sure you *go* before you go."

The other Rutgers story Jim was fond of was often told at clinics. He also made it a part of his final speech at the ESPYs in 1993, two months before his death:

> When I first started coaching, my idol was Vince Lombardi. I read everything I could about Lombardi. One of my favorite stories was how, when he first got the job in Green Bay, he made such a great impression on the team before his first game.
>
> Most pregame talks become kind of routine for coaches. We keep them on index cards, know them pretty much by heart, and pull out the one we need depending on the situation. We

get the team together about a half an hour before we're ready to take the field or court and start the speech. Speech No. 7, got it right here.

Not Lombardi though. This game he just waited in the hall outside the locker room. Fifteen minutes till game time . . . ten minutes . . . five minutes, but still no Lombardi. The players were wondering, "Where is he? He's supposed to be this great coach and he's not even in the locker room before we take the field?"

Finally, with only a couple of minutes left, Lombardi came bursting through the door. We all remember what a great presence he had. There was complete silence as he looked around at the players with all eyes focused intently on him. "Gentlemen," he said, "we will be successful this year if you make important to you three things and three things only: your religion, your family, and the Green Bay Packers." That was it. That's all he said, and with that they charged onto the field to victory, and the rest is history.

I decided to do the same thing before my first game. I was so fired up! I practiced the speech over and over. "Gentlemen, we'll be successful this year if you make important to you three things, and three things only: your religion, your family, and Rutgers basketball."

I was ready. On the night of the first game I was waiting in the hall like Lombardi. Fifteen minutes . . . ten minutes . . . the manager was saying, "C'mon, coach, we have to go in." "No, no. Not yet."

Finally, like Lombardi, with a few minutes left, I decided it was time to burst through the doors. But they wouldn't open! I crashed into them so hard that I almost broke my arm! I hit them again, harder this time, and then I went sailing through, lost my balance, and wound up sprawled on the floor with my players having to help me up.

Undaunted, picking up the pieces of my dignity and rubbing my sore arm, I started pacing back and forth till all eyes were on me and I had their undivided attention. The kids were already excited—it was their first game! They were 19, I was only 22, but I was going to light a fire underneath all of them and motivate them like they'd never been before. This was my big moment. "Gentlemen," I began, "we will be successful this year if you make important to you three things, and three things only." Heads nodded eagerly in agreement and anticipation. "Your religion, your family, and *the Green Bay Packers!*"

Dead silence. I don't know if it inspired them for the game, but at least three of them became lifelong Packer fans.

Jim learned from these humble beginnings as well as from working with a consummate professional like Bill Foster. Foster had a very successful career as a head coach at Rutgers, Utah, Duke, South Carolina, and Northwestern, and was a great visionary about many of the organizational and business aspects of coaching. In short, he taught Jim to take what you *do* very seriously, but not to take *yourself* too seriously. This helped him to connect with people. We all want to feel that what we are doing is valuable and worthwhile, but we also enjoy finding humor in those things that we can all relate to, which reminds us not to take ourselves too seriously.

After Rutgers, Jim moved on to Johns Hopkins University. He was there for only one year, but it was his first head coaching job, and he found that he had an aptitude for the profession. They had not had a winning season in 24 years, and even though they were only 10–9 during his year there, a winning season is a winning season. He had done his part to turn the program around.

Having played and coached sports all his life, Jim took the importance of winning for granted. But once during a road trip, some of his players came up from the back of the bus to ask him a question. These were student-athletes in the real sense of the term, kids who were getting an education in order to become doctors, lawyers, and other professionals, and who played basketball for the enjoyment of the game and the competition. "Excuse me, coach," they said, "we've been in the back of the bus discussing you, and what we want to know is, why is winning so important to you?" That brought Jim up short, almost as if he had never thought about it before, and from the number of times he told this story, I know it changed his attitude and perspective for the rest of his life. (Of course, as Jim said, it's easy to keep things in perspective when, as the head basketball coach, assistant football coach, and head freshman baseball coach, your most important job is acting as the *ticket manager* of the nationally ranked lacrosse team.)

When he went to University of Connecticut, Jim worked for one of college basketball's great treasures, Dee Rowe, known throughout New England simply as Dee. It's hard to find anyone to say anything bad about Dee, especially in New England, where he was a legendary prep school coach before going to the University of Connecticut Huskies. He had a humanity about him that Jim immediately loved and admired. Jim wanted very much to emulate Dee if and when *he* became a Division I head coach. Said Dee:

> When I brought Jim here, I fell in love with him. He had an insatiable passion for the game and for life. Everything about him was magic, and I could see he was very special early on.

Like Jim, Dee had a passion, a deep, consuming passion for the game and for coaching it. One of Jim's biggest jobs, he often said only half-kiddingly, was talking Dee down off the roof after losses. As Dee jokingly admitted:

> I used to kid James—which is what I always called him—that in my 21 years as a head coach, the only two losing seasons I had were with him as my assistant. Those were two rough years, and he kept me from jumping in the Connecticut River more than once.

This terrific coach, this nice man, this loving father and great friend, was absolutely consumed with the game throughout his career, and it often would just eat him up. Why? Why was winning so important? Dee Rowe had the passion that Jim felt a coach ought to have, that he himself wanted to have, but how to answer the question on the bus from the Johns Hopkins players? Why was winning so important?

Part of the answer came in a painful way. One day the coaches at UConn received a letter from the parents of a boy in the hospital whose condition was grave. He had been a passionate UConn basketball fan since the time he could talk. He listened to every game on the radio and remembered in great detail each of the handful of games he had been able to attend. His parents had a humble request. Could the team members all sign a basketball and send it to their son in the hospital?

This letter moved Dee and his entire staff, and they decided they could do better. They autographed a basketball, and then the whole staff and most of the team went to the hospital to personally deliver it. The young man got to meet and talk to all the players and coaches and was given many other autographed items in addition to the ball. It was apparent that he was just thrilled, and his parents were overwhelmed. As a final gift, the team told the boy that they would dedicate their next game to him. Since he always listened on the radio, he would hear it announced that the Huskies—*his* Huskies—were playing for him.

If this were a movie script, UConn would have gone out and won the next game and the young boy, inspired, would have made a miraculous recovery and gone on to do great things with his life. It didn't work out that way. UConn lost a heartbreaker by two points and the young man died just two weeks later. He was only 10 years old.

A few weeks later a letter to the coaching staff arrived in which the boy's parents thanked the coaches and the players for all they had done, and told them how much it had meant to their son. It concluded: "Please let all your players and coaches know that thanks to their time and kindness, the last two weeks of a little boy's life were happy ones."

Jim had just had his first daughter, Nicole, two years earlier. He was amazed to think that these parents, who must have been absolutely devastated, would take the time to thank a basketball team and their coaches. It helped him to understand that there was something very special about being a college coach or athlete. He carried that letter with him for the rest of his life.

This experience also began to show him where that elusive balance is between the passion for winning and the ability to keep it in perspective. He realized that winning isn't everything, but *trying* to win, and doing your best, very nearly is. He was fond of citing this quotation from Teddy Roosevelt:

> In the battle of life, it is not the critic who counts, not the man who points out how the strong man stumbled or where the doer of deeds may have done better. The credit belongs to the man who is in the arena, whose face is marred by dust and sweat and blood; who errs and comes short again and again, for there is no effort without error and shortcoming; who, if he succeeds, knows the triumph of high achievement; but who, if he fails, at least fails while daring greatly, so that his place shall never be with those cold and timid souls who know neither victory nor defeat.

Through that quotation and his own example, Jim burned into me the desire to be "in the arena" and not one of the "cold and timid souls who know neither victory nor defeat." I have sometimes been embarrassed by the fact that I seem to idolize my older brother. Not because I feel strongly about him, but because I sense that people think I do it for the wrong reasons. They think it's because he was a successful coach and broadcaster who rubbed shoulders with celebrities, and that I was awestruck by his success and wanted it for myself. The truth is, while I found great pleasure in Jim's success and was appropriately excited at the prospects of sharing in some of his star-studded experiences, I went into coaching and later broadcasting because I enjoyed those fields and felt I had a talent for them. Period. More important, I felt the way I did about Jim because he was my big brother; anyone who has a big brother they look up to can understand that.

Bucknell proved to be, not surprisingly, a challenge. The Bisons were a combined 20–49 in the three years prior to Jim's arrival in 1972, including 5–18 the previous year. They had won more than 13 games in a season only once since 1958–1959. It wasn't exactly a basketball hotbed, and as such, not exactly in great demand among recruits. Two players Jim did manage to recruit tell interesting stories of how they wound up at Bucknell. Roger Clark recalls his first meeting with Jim:

> V was in Washington, D.C., to recruit some other players, and saw me play. I played at McKinley Tech, which is in kind of a rough part of town. While the game was going on, someone broke into Coach Valvano's car and stole his briefcase. Right after that, he came to our house to recruit me. Now, here is this man who we don't know from Adam, and he has just been robbed, not far from my home. Yet the instant he was in our home he just connected. My father really liked him. Jim just acted like he "belonged" with us. I liked him right away and was happy that my parents did too.

Thomas McLean remembers his experience a little differently:

> I was going to Blair Academy, and was a successful track athlete as well as basketball player. But basketball was my first love. I had already decided I didn't want to run track in college, but I was going to play basketball. And I was a bit wild. I

remember we played a game where we lost 64–39, and I had 32 of the 39 points. I was celebrating after I scored, slapping hands with the crowd like we were winning! And people *were* paying attention. . . . I remember Dick Vitale, who was at Rutgers at the time, trying to recruit me, and Bill Foster, who was then at Utah. But I didn't care, I had already decided I was going to play for Tark [Jerry Tarkanian] at Long Beach State. I was a runner, and a goalie, and I was sick of the cold. I wanted to play hoops, and go somewhere warm, and I *was* going to Long Beach State. Period.

My mom had other ideas; she wanted me to go to Williams, or Tufts, maybe Lehigh. She wanted a good academic school. Me? I wanted to play with Ed Ratliff for Tark.

Well, Coach V comes to our house to recruit me. All the other coaches who came in would sit in the dining room and wait while my mother cooked a little something to eat. Not Jim. He came right in the kitchen and started talking. Now that's important, you have to understand. In an African American household, there is something intimate about sitting in the kitchen. V felt comfortable doing that right away, and I could tell my mom really loved the guy.

She kept telling him, "You know, my son is quite a handful." And I was. I was into Jimi Hendrix and was wearing the headbands and all that wild tie-dye stuff. And V just kept saying, "He'll do fine at Bucknell. We'll make sure he gets a good education." I was standing behind him, waving at my mother. "No! The Susquehanna Valley! Cold! Snow! No way! I'm going to Long Beach . . . Tark . . . Ed Ratliff!"

After Jim left I said, "Mom, you're not falling for all that, are you?" And she just said, "You know, I really like that Jim Valvano." I said, "*Jim* Valvano? Oh, it's like that, huh? You're on a first-name basis with him now?" But she was a school administrator, and she really liked and respected Coach V. That's when I knew I was headed for Lewisburg.

It was a bumpy road during Jim's first two years at Bucknell. After a good leap forward in his first year (to 11–14), they dropped to 8–16 in year two. Then in year three, with Roger Clark doing lots of the blue-collar work—rebounding and defending—Jim started what became a trend for him: building around guards. Tom McLean was joined by Gerald Purnell as well as other talented players like Sam Stettler and Scott Hebditch. Year three looked promising.

It didn't start that way, however. They started the year 1–6. After back-to-back wins, both McLean and Clark point to the next game as the real turnaround. "We were playing Pitt at home, and they were good, just coming off a postseason bid. But by now we understood how Coach V wanted us to play, and he was figuring out how to get us to do that," said Clark. "He was great at understanding human nature," added McLean. "And he would resort to unusual circumstances to make his point."

Both men recall an incident in that Pitt game, retold here by McLean:

> We were just kicking their ass in the first half, really just taking the ball at them and driving right by them. The second half started and they started making a run at us. The lead was dwindling. It was just about almost gone, and V took a timeout.
>
> This was what he had been working for. He had a good team, and he had upgraded the schedule. We'd played at South Carolina, at Penn State. Now we had a good team in Pitt, at home, and we were beating them. And we were letting it slip away!
>
> He was so angry, he called timeout, and he just got in the huddle, and he was so pissed off he couldn't even speak. He was just moving his arms, and pacing in a little circle, and making noises, like grunts. No words were coming out, just sounds.
>
> Now, Roger Clark, Gerald Purnell, and myself were sitting side by side on the bench, and the whole timeout was just about over. He still hadn't said anything understandable. He finally took his hand and, like Moe used to do with the other two stooges, slapped all three of us in one swipe across the face!
>
> Now the three of us were city kids with a tough side, and we got up, really ready to kick his [Jimmy's] ass! Right there on the bench! And he looked at the expression on our faces, glared at each of us, and said, "*That's* the kind of emotion I need out *there!*" and he pointed to the court. That was the whole timeout.

"We went out there and beat Pitt 72–66," concluded McLean.

Said Clark about the incident:

> It didn't really hurt us, but it was so out of character for him
> that it woke us up. I mean, he was very emotional, but he was
> usually so analytical. . . . It was all the more powerful for that
> reason. We went on from there, put together a nine-game win-
> ning streak, and were being talked about for a possible NIT bid
> late in the year.

With a 14–12 mark posted against an upgraded schedule, Bucknell
was in fact getting some attention, and Roger Clark wasn't surprised
when, shortly after the season, opportunity knocked for Jim:

> He [Valvano] called us in and talked to us individually about
> the possibility of going to Iona College. I knew he was from
> New York, and knew Bucknell wasn't going to keep him long.
> He asked me if I wanted to come with him, but I had really
> become comfortable at Bucknell and wanted to stay. I had
> some academic problems my first year, but Coach V told me
> he was sure I could do the work and had some of the upper-
> classmen help me along a bit. I was doing well now academi-
> cally, and wanted to graduate from Bucknell, so I stayed.

Tom McLean's story is quite different:

> He told us he was offered the Iona job, and I said, "Let's go.
> I'm coming with you." But he said something that really turned
> me around. He said, "Thomas, you know what I see when I
> watch you run down the floor? I see something beautiful. You
> need to stay here and you need to run again. [Track Coach]
> Art Gulden is a good guy. . . . You should run for him, and get
> to know him. Besides I promised your mother you'd get your
> degree from here and you should stay and do that." I walked
> away and said to myself, "I just got turned down!" But it never
> felt so good getting rejected before. And I stayed.
>   As Coach V said, Coach Gulden, who I really didn't see eye
> to eye with at the start, did turn out to be a good guy, and became
> a good friend. I have stayed in touch with him all my life.

Thomas McLean did in fact run, becoming one of the world's best 880 runners; he went on to represent the United States on the Pan Am team and later to hold an executive position at USA Track & Field. Roger Clark and Gerald Purnell also went on to successful professional lives; Clark is a district sales manager for Pfizer and Purnell is a lawyer in Washington, D.C.

Bucknell University would also go on to great success on the hardwood, first under Charlie Woolum and then with current coach Pat Flannery. "His successors have had great success at Bucknell, but Jim was the one who first got the program noticed, brought some excitement to it, and put Bucknell basketball on the map," said Roger Clark.

/ / /

Two things Jim did for me during this time made a lasting impression on me, and I will never forget them. One was an overheard remark, the other an incident that might be called "crisis at the junior prom." When I was 14, Jim had just finished his first year at Bucknell and the family was there visiting him, Pam, and Nicole. I was at that awkward age where I could find a way to say or do something stupid in almost any situation: at dinner, with guests, anywhere. I suppose it's a normal part of growing up, but at the time I had very little self-esteem and often felt like a complete clod. I happened to overhear my mom and Jim talking about going somewhere and whether or not I should be included. Jim said, "I hope we can take him, because I really like the kid."

Quick, put down the book for a minute! Stop and think about how that would make a 14-year-old kid with low self-esteem feel, to hear that from his big brother, whom he not only looked up to but also idolized. If you could bottle confidence and inject it in a vein it wouldn't have made me feel any better about myself!

A couple of years later, when I was in the 11th grade, I asked a girl to the junior prom. I thought she said no so I didn't buy any tickets, but it turned out that she thought she had said yes, and proceeded to buy *everything*—a dress, shoes, and all the accessories. Word got back to me that she thought we were going, and I panicked because I knew there were no tickets left. Sold out. No way. I was humiliated beyond belief and spent the last couple of weeks of the school year pretty depressed.

When you're 16, everyone tries to make you feel better by telling you that whatever it is that's bothering you is no big deal. I remember that advice making me feel worse. I was still embarrassed about the dance and now, evidently, I was also an idiot for feeling bad about it!

Jim invited me to Lewisburg for the weekend. He took me to a little deli for dinner and gave me some advice I still use today. There was a repeated checkerboard tile pattern on the floor. The middle white tiles each touched four other black tiles at their corners. Jim said:

> I hear you feel pretty bad. I heard what happened, and you *should* feel bad. That's pretty embarrassing for you. Let me tell you *why* you feel bad. You see that tile in the middle? That represents something important in your life, let's say school. The tiles around it are all the things that go with school like friends, sports, and proms. When that middle square is bad, it makes all the others tough to deal with too, since you can't separate them.
>
> What I want to tell you is, everyone has something embarrassing happen to them at one time or another. I do; we all do. The difference is, I have more of those boxes. I have a box labeled "coach" and it touches four other boxes. But then I also have "father," "husband," "friend," "camp director," and "radio host" boxes, and each of those boxes touch four *other* boxes that are different from the rest. When I get to feeling bad about one of my boxes—say Pam and I have a fight—I can lose myself in one of my other ones. I can go to the "coach" box and lose myself in work at the office.
>
> You are 16, and you can't do that. You have no job to go to, no car to go there in, no friends, really, that are outside school. It's *harder for you*, and people who tell you not to worry about it, that there's plenty of fish in the sea or other clichés, don't really understand that. Don't be mad at them; they mean well, but they just don't get it, and they're trying to make you feel better.
>
> I don't think I can do that. So all I can say is that you're going to feel bad for a while. That's the way it is. But something odd is going to happen. Tomorrow, when you wake up, look out the window. The sun will be up there, no matter how you feel. And eventually, if you hang in there, you'll have a chance to add more boxes to your life. Even now—basketball camps, summer leagues, summer jobs—all new boxes. And one day you'll decide you don't want to feel bad about that first box

anymore and, after enough sunrises, things will be OK for you. When? I don't know. Next week, next month, but it *will* happen. Just hang in there.

I walked out of there feeling better immediately. We went back to his house and Jim and Pam invited another couple over. They let me try a mixed drink called a grasshopper, and I had never even had a beer! They included me in the conversation, and for at least one night I had new friends who acted as if I were an adult like them, not a cloddy 16-year-old with junior prom troubles.

Then we got a phone call telling me that the student elections, which were held that day, and for which I had submitted my name weeks before when I was feeling better, were over—and I had won! My school "box" now had a shiny new addition attached to it, one I could feel good about after I was done experiencing this great "little brother" box in Pennsylvania.

By the way, if you want to hear the junior prom story told from a different perspective, you can ask my wife Darlene about it. She's the girl I thought had turned me down.

I wasn't the only youngster Jim was influencing during his days at Bucknell. He spent most of his summer speaking at basketball camps and clinics in the Northeast, often more than one a day. He'd average well over 150 talks at various camps, including his own, during the summer months and got to know a great many coaches. At his own camp he had terrific speakers like Jim Lynam, Tom Davis, George Raveling, and Chuck Daly. He had a lot of fun at his camps, but between the softball games, miniature golf tournaments, and midnight "hoagie runs," the emphasis was always on teaching, instruction, and sound basketball fundamentals.

He told his campers that the outside speakers who visited were in great demand at basketball camps all over and that it was up to them, the campers, to make sure they got a better lecture than that same speaker might deliver elsewhere. How? By being enthusiastic! Sit up straight, pay attention, answer questions, and hustle onto the court when he asks for volunteers. Hey, this guy was going to give the same clinic down the road at a competing camp, and you might play those guys in a game next season. Let's get a *better* lecture than they do! Start when the speaker is introduced. Don't just applaud politely; give him a standing ovation! When he tells you to sit down, keep standing and yell and clap all the louder!

This technique worked a little bit too well one summer when I happened to be there as a camper. Jim introduced the speaker and we all went absolutely berserk. Guys were stamping their feet, whistling, yelling, and just wouldn't quit. The coach got a little embarrassed, looked at Jim, smiled, and signaled for us all to sit down. But no! We were not to be denied. We kept on cheering, the decibel level getting louder and louder. The speaker was now a little dumbfounded and really didn't know what to do; he tried to get Jim to quiet us down. But even he couldn't quiet his own campers. With the noise getting louder and louder, all of a sudden Jim took off and started running victory laps around the gym with his arms waving triumphantly above his head, egging us on. Now the place was really going crazy, and he ran right out of the gym!

Davis Gym at Bucknell is a great old arena, with several entrance tunnels on each side on both the upper and lower levels. The campers were all still yelling and cheering as loud as ever, but they were also looking everywhere. Where's V? Finally, after about a minute, he came back in through a tunnel on the upper level, and the place erupted again. He ran along the upper stands and then—zip!—back out via a different exit. Now everyone was looking, still cheering the whole time, with the stunned speaker just standing there. And then there's Jim again! A new roar arose as Jim came back in . . . then out again . . . then back in. He did this about four times, and each time the cheering got louder when he reappeared. Finally he made his way back to the floor level, picked up a ball, and dribbled the length of the court. He tried to dunk, which he couldn't do, spiked the ball into the ground, and fell down, exhausted.

I want to tell you, that crowd was *warmed up*! We got that speaker's "A" game, no doubt about that. The routine went over so well that Jim used it again and again every time he introduced a speaker at his camp. It finally got to be so well known that when he introduced Jim Lynam, Lynam grabbed Jimmy to stop his run and did it himself instead!

With the contacts he had made and the success he had had at Bucknell, Jim got some fairly high-profile offers, including one from an ambitious college in New York with a president who, like Jim, dreamed great dreams, and saw a stronger basketball program as part of what he was trying to achieve for the school. New Rochelle, New York, was the next rung on the coaching ladder for Jim, and it gave him one of his favorite introductory lines: "Hi, I'm Jim Valvano. Iona College."

7

IONA

IT COULDN'T HAVE BEEN EASY MOVING FROM AN IDYLLIC AND picturesque university setting in the rolling hills of western Pennsylvania to an urban campus whose centerpiece was a multilevel parking garage, but that's exactly what the Valvano family did when they went from Bucknell to Iona in 1975. But the gritty Iona campus had one great thing going for it in Jim's mind: it was near New York City, and that meant it was near Madison Square Garden, the center of the basketball universe.

Like the NIT, the Garden held a lure and fascination for an earlier generation of basketball players and fans that is hard to overstate. It had a storied, and indeed almost magical, history, from the great CCNY teams of Nat Holman in the fifties to the excitement that accompanied Hank Luisetti as he came cross country from Stanford with his revolutionary one-handed shot. Jim had been going there since he was a kid, watching our dad ref games, and from the moment he set foot on the Iona campus, his dream was to take his team to play in the featured 9:00 game of a Garden doubleheader in front of a packed house.

As it happened, the president of the college, Brother James Driscoll, was a visionary who knew his school needed more exposure in the metropolitan area. They were competing with other fine Catholic institutions such as Fordham, Manhattan, St. Francis, Marist, and St. John's, and he was sure that a revitalized basketball program would not only be a way of attracting new students, but would also bring many of the existing ones, who were mostly commuters, back to campus at night. And it *was* a program in need of some revitalization, since they were 4–19 the previous year. For Jim's part, he was sure there were plenty of good players in the New York area who would share his dream of building a great program at

Iona, and he was right. Three in particular had a big impact and contributed to the success he had in New Rochelle.

The first was Dave Brown. When Jim got the job it was too late to do much recruiting, and he was quite fortunate to have a chance to see Brown play and then to recruit him successfully. He was the player that made Iona competitive during Jim's very first year, leading them to an 11–15 record.

Jim once went to see Brown play in some all-star game in New Jersey. It was a classic recruiting day. The game was run, if you can use that term, not by a school but by some outside group. It was scheduled for 1:00 P.M. We got there at about 12:30. We did not know that there was a preliminary game, which didn't start until close to 2:00. It was soon apparent that no one in the prelim game was going to help get Iona into the Garden. Then came the between-game entertainment. It went on for about an hour and a half! Karate demonstrations, gymnastics. We did get to see a guy break about six boards with his head, which was cool. While the preliminary game bored Jimmy, the karate exhibition fascinated him. The show was pretty good itself, but Jim's comments made it even more entertaining. He kept up a running commentary with the entire bleacher section. Keep in mind, this is before North Carolina State and TV fame— these people had no idea who Jim was. But he pretty much took over the stands with his joking, much to the amusement of the other spectators. Dave Brown played in the second game. He was about 6'6" and was clearly a better caliber than the players in the first game.

Brown also made it possible for Jim to go after higher-profile players, including the second key recruit he landed, Glenn Vickers. Vickers was perhaps the most talented player on Long Island, and was recruited literally all across the country; the University of San Francisco was one of his final options. He chose Iona, giving the little school instant credibility with every blue-chip prospect in the country. With Vickers and a great recruiting class that included another terrific guard named Kevin Hamilton, Iona had a winning season immediately.

But more important, those recruits put Iona in a position to land the biggest prize of all, a signing that rocked the college basketball world. Jeff Ruland was a 6'10" center who was on everyone's All-America list. His recruitment sounded like a Who's Who list of suitors—Indiana, North Carolina, Notre Dame, Kentucky—literally hundreds of colleges across the country in every major conference. Oh, and also Iona. This was in an era when there were far fewer restrictions on how often a coach could see a prospect play or practice, and for all intents and purposes, someone from Iona was there virtually every single day of Ruland's senior year.

Ruland kept eliminating big names off his list, paring it down, and Iona's name kept getting mentioned. Kentucky really wanted him. A rumor floated around that a wealthy Wildcat booster, baffled by Ruland's strong feelings for Iona, asked him, "How 'bout I buy it and we'll make it a UK satellite campus?"

Bob Knight was also trying hard to land Ruland, and at one point he said to Jim, "Listen, if Jeff eliminates us, I'll push him to you, and if he eliminates Iona, you push him to us." Knight also suspected that Kentucky was cheating during the process; when Ruland signed a letter of intent for Iona, Knight may have felt that they were cheating too. That's the only explanation Jim could think of for why Knight was so outspoken in his criticism when Jim was having his problems at North Carolina State.

Regardless, Ruland did wind up at Iona, and he was a great, great player. Big and strong, he understood how to play, too, and with great guards like Vickers and Hamilton, Iona had three national-caliber players. They added some other talented kids as well, like Mike Palma, who transferred from Wake Forest; Alex Middleton and Kevin Vesey, two other quality big men; good New York City recruits Lester George and Glenn McMillan; and another fine guard from Pennsylvania, Tony Iati. All these kids were highly regarded and helped make Iona a program of national prominence. Players of this caliber got peoples' attention quickly, and basketball insiders soon realized that Iona was a force to be reckoned with.

What attracted these talented players and held them together was their common pursuit of "the dream." "Dare to Dream" became Iona's theme. Ruland has since stated in no uncertain terms that the reason he chose Iona was that he believed he could stay near home and still make the dream of a national championship come true. He and Jimmy could be the ones to *make* that happen; he didn't need to jump on board an existing powerhouse. They could *create* a powerhouse and win it all! A national championship! At Iona! This is instructive, and represents a key element in Jim's personality. He aimed as high as he could possibly aim—the national championship—even with a small school like Iona, and as a result he was successful. And he didn't just *aim* high. He really believed in his heart, and got his players to believe, that they *could* win it all, even at tiny Iona College.

As astonishing as that goal might have been, it was only the tip of the
iceberg according to Rich Petriccione, who became Jim's student manager
when he was 18 and in his freshman year:

> One of the first things I ever did with V was take a scouting trip
> to Fairleigh Dickenson University in New Jersey. This was my
> first year on the staff as a student manager, and V brought me
> along to do the driving. It was about an hour drive, tops, and I
> had never really spent any time with him yet, so I really didn't
> know him well at all. We started driving, and by the time we got
> to New Jersey he had told me all this incredible stuff he planned
> to do: win the 9:00 game in the Garden, win the national
> championship, get in the Basketball Hall of Fame, be on *The
> Tonight Show*, make a million dollars, coach the Knicks, and I'm
> thinking to myself, "This guy is nuts!" I mean, we just struggled
> to beat Pace about two nights earlier, now we got a "big one"
> coming up with Buffalo! And we're going to win the 9:00 game
> in the Garden? A national championship? *The Tonight Show*, for
> God's sake? I really thought he was completely crazy.
>
> For some reason, Coach really took a liking to me, and tried
> to include me in almost everything involved in the program.
> We'd go on the road, and he'd hang out with me! I like to think
> it was because I would listen to him talk. And talk . . . and talk
> . . . but he really wanted to hear what you had to say as well. He
> asked me during that first trip to FDU, "What's your dream?
> What do *you* want to do with your life? You have to know these
> things, Pet. Because if not, remember the wisdom of Yogi Berra,
> who said, 'If you don't know where it is you're going, and you get
> lost, you might wind up someplace else.' Remember that, Pet."
>
> And he would ask your opinion on just about any topic as
> well. If you gave a good, intelligent answer, he would listen and
> it would help shape his opinion of you, and the topic in dis-
> cussion. But, whatever you did, you didn't want to sound stu-
> pid! That would open you up to incredible ridicule, and he
> really didn't want to hear what you had to say, maybe ever. For
> V, the bottom line always was intelligence. He couldn't care
> less what you did, or what your station in life was, but if you
> were intelligent, you were in his inner circle.

That inner circle was something that people definitely wanted to be included in. People wanted to hang around V; there's no question about that. And V would be happy to accommodate them. He would just take over a room or a situation, and to me, those were the funniest moments. His "packaged" material—you know, "the son of Rocco and Angelina" and all that—that was all good and funny, don't get me wrong, but the improvised things were what you remembered most and were make-your-sides-hurt funny.

I remember we played in San Francisco, and V wanted the players to have a chance to see the local culture in the city. He arranged a tour bus to take the players through the city. We got to the bus, and the only ones on it were a few boosters, V, Tony Iati, and myself. Doesn't matter, we were going to go anyway. The tour guide started and he was one of those monotone, "if-you-look-to-your-left-you'll-see . . ." kind of guides. Very dull. Definitely not for V. Finally, when we were in the markets by the piers, V couldn't take it anymore. He took over the microphone and started in. At that time, Dan Ackroyd was doing a bit on *Saturday Night Live* that was pretty big. It was a takeoff on those kitchen gadget TV ads. Ackroyd "sold" the "Bass-o-Matic" where, in staccato style, he told you all the benefits of putting bass and other fish into a blender. It was a popular, funny bit. Well, V looked out and saw fish being sold as far as the eye could see on either side of the bus and he started in, sounding exactly like Ackroyd. "Now you can get every type of fish ever discovered! That's right—every type of fish found in the world can be *yours* right here in San Francisco! You get tuna, sturgeon, bass, mackerel, cod, roughy, trout, barracuda, snapper, goldfish, clown fish, catfish, jellyfish . . ." He was running out of fish. "Help me out, Pet! Gimme some other fish!" "Pike," I said. "Pike!" V said, clearly pleased. And he went on like that for about five minutes. People who were there still talk about V and the "fish routine" in San Francisco. It was *really* funny. And all improvised.

Back home, Jim was on the biggest stage in the world—New York— and he was more than happy to talk to anyone who would listen about his shiny new team at Iona. After a losing season in year one, the Gaels had a winning year with Vickers and Hamilton as freshmen, going 15–10, including a win over St. John's, easily the most dominant of the metropolitan New York teams. That got peoples' attention. Then they had an even better year when they added Jeff Ruland, going 17–10, and just missed qualifying for the NCAA tournament when they lost by three points to St. John's in the ECAC tournament. The Gael fans attending that game, which was played in the Nassau Coliseum on Long Island, serenaded their team after the *loss* with a chant of "Thank you Gaels! Thank you Gaels!" It was a classy and heartwarming gesture. It was obvious that Iona basketball was becoming something special.

Even though Iona was beginning to achieve some national prominence, Jim continued to take pleasure in the less-heralded aspects of the program, as he always had. One of his players, Lester George, was struggling a bit in the classroom. He was from a fine high school in Brooklyn called Bishop Loughlin, but was having a difficult time during his first two years. He was trying hard, however, and Jim believed he had the ability to make it academically. Toward the end of the year, Jim was sitting in his office on the day grades were due to be posted and sent out. All of a sudden, unannounced, just sticking his head in the office door, there was Lester George. He leaned in and said simply, "I'm just here to tell you, Lester George is going to be a junior!" And with that he was off.

Jim's relish in repeating that story showed he had a real concern for his players and for academics, beyond just the chest thumping many coaches do as they point to their graduation rates. Beginning at least with his head coaching job at Bucknell, he always made it a priority to have upperclassmen help freshmen who were struggling. While he was at Bucknell he helped me in another way, and taught me a lesson I've never forgotten.

I was in high school at the time, and every summer I attended the Long Island Lutheran basketball camp. My dad had run the camp for many years, and Jim was now on the staff there, and so for four years I spent six weeks there every summer. One day the courts were being prepared for a shooting contest that was scheduled after lunch. A few of us got there early and were fooling around, not really concentrating or seriously preparing for the contest, and none of us really shot well. I know I didn't.

That afternoon, as we were driving home, Jim said, "Boy, you really struggled in the shooting contest today." Since in the actual contest I had done OK, I was taken aback. "What are you talking about? I didn't win, but I wasn't bad." Jim said, "I'm not talking about the contest itself, I'm talking about during lunch. You missed about eight shots in a row." I protested that we were just goofing around, that they didn't really count, I wasn't trying, all sorts of lame excuses. Jim said, "That's true, but I was sitting in the shade under a tree with [a prominent local college coach] and he said, 'Your brother isn't a bad player, but he doesn't shoot real well, does he?'" I said, "We weren't even playing!" And Jim said something I later incorporated into my entire coaching career. He said, "Remember this: every time you step between the lines, someone will be watching you. They don't know if you're goofing around, or trying, or sick, or tired, or hurt. All they know is what they see. When you are between those lines, assume somebody important is watching and ask yourself, 'What are they thinking of how I'm playing? *Today. Right now.*'"

Years later I read that people asked Joe DiMaggio why he always seemed so intense no matter who the opposition was, no matter how dominant the Yankees were. His response was similar to Jim's advice: "There might be somebody in the stands who is seeing me play for the first time that day, maybe the only time. I owe it to that guy to do my best."

In Jim's fourth year at Iona, they won 20 games and once again faced St. John's in the ECAC championship game. Again the game was played at Nassau Coliseum on Long Island, home of the Valvano family, as well as of Vickers, Hamilton, Ruland, Vesey, and Palma. It might as well have been a home game for Iona. This time they beat them and gained their first ever berth in the NCAA tournament. The Long Island newspaper, *Newsday*, obviously had many great local angles, not the least of which was how longtime Long Island coach and teacher Rocky Valvano was there to watch his son achieve one of his dreams.

The next year, Jim's fifth and last at Iona, saw them record what was without a doubt the biggest victory in the history of the school. It was February 21, 1980, and Iona was playing the University of Louisville in the 9:00 game of a Madison Square Garden doubleheader, making another of Jim's most cherished dreams a reality. The Cardinals, under legendary coach Denny Crum, had a great team, with Rodney and Scooter McCray, Darrell Griffith, Jerry Eaves, Wiley Brown, and Derek Smith. The first game had featured P. J. Carlesimo's Wagner team against Ray Meyer's DePaul University squad, so it was a hot ticket. Iona came into the game with a record of 23–4, and were 11 games into a winning streak that would reach 17 games. They already had some Garden games under their belt and had upgraded their schedule to include teams like Kentucky, Kansas,

Long Beach State, San Francisco, and Georgetown, so playing in front of 19,000 screaming fans was nothing new. But the outcome, a thrilling 77–60 victory against one of the best teams in the country, was the stuff dreams are made of. I will never forget the image of Jim racing back and forth in front of his bench, punching the air in a feverish euphoria, while I joined in the yelling and screaming, more excited than I had ever been watching a game before. It was the last game the U of L lost that year, as they went on to win the national championship.

The Gaels went on to make their second straight NCAA appearance, and won their first-round game against Holy Cross. Next up was Georgetown, for the right to make it to the "Sweet 16," and easily the biggest game in Iona history. It was a close game but the Hoyas had the upper hand until Iona made a late run. Finally, down by a point with only seconds remaining, Glenn Vickers missed a jump shot that would have given Iona the lead, and Georgetown closed them out, 74–71.

After the game, a number of reporters were impressed by the poise of the Iona players, especially Vickers, who, when asked about the emotion and pressure of taking that last shot and what must have gone through his mind, calmly said he was not intimidated for one reason. "I was recruited to take that shot," he said simply.

That comment spoke volumes about what all the players and coaches should have been proud of. First, when Vickers was recruited, the thought that Iona would be *in* the NCAA tournament would have been laughable. But he and all his teammates believed it, because the guy in charge believed it and, more important, believed in *them*. They also believed that not only would they be in the tournament but that they would make that shot and win once they got there. They did win that first-round game— Iona's first ever NCAA tournament win—and if you press people like Jeff Ruland, currently the highly successful head coach at Iona, they will tell you that if Glenn had made that shot, they might not have lost again.

Jeff Ruland was raised in a single-parent, blue-collar household on Long Island. His mother ran a bar for years, gave no quarter to anyone, and much of her shoot-from-the-hip, tell-it-like-it-is attitude toward life rubbed off on her son. When Ruland arrived at Iona he was streetwise, gruff, and a little rough around the edges, but he had a heart as big as all outdoors. He valued loyalty and friendship above all else, and wanted to deal with people who were as direct and forthright as his mother. He was also a dreamer, and believed as strongly in Jim's dream as Jim himself did:

I went to Iona for a few reasons. The first was it was close to home, but still a place I believed could win a national championship. I really believed it—in fact, if I hadn't played the last part of my junior year with two broken hands, I think we would have been a Final Four team that year. We beat Louisville by 17 points and they won the national championship. But I also went because Jimmy was so damn honest with me. I was getting recruited by all these schools, and I remember a game in high school where I played terribly. I mean I just really stunk—the ball was bouncing off my hands, out of bounds. After the game, all these other recruiters came up to me and said the usual crap. You know, "Hey Jeff, nice game . . . loved watching you play . . . you were great." V came down after the game and said, "Damn, you really sucked tonight." And I did! I liked that about him. That's what my mother would have told me, and it was true.

The other reason I went really had to do with our friendship. I thought of Jimmy as a friend. And we spent a lot of time together. My senior year I took official visits to Wake Forest, North Carolina, Kentucky, Notre Dame, and Indiana, and every week I took an unofficial trip to Iona. Every week . . . and Jimmy and I would just have fun. He was as wild as I was. We would go play Split Rock Golf Course in New Rochelle and after four holes, we'd lose interest in the game. We'd be racing the golf carts, playing polo golf, where you hit the ball without getting out of the cart. One time, V had to go into the woods for a nature call, and I didn't see him for about two minutes. Next thing I look up and there he is, buck naked! Another round I drove the damn cart into a lake. The course manager must have liked us though, because he kept letting us come back.

It was always like that with Jim. We had fun together, and I felt that if I went to Iona, we would still have fun together. I mean, if Jimmy wasn't at Iona, I probably would have gone to Kentucky, but they had won the championship without me. They didn't need me. I could win a championship, stay near home, and play for—and play *with*—V.

And it really was fun. I mean after games, we would go to Joey De Fonz's place, and V and the coaches would be there, and the players would come in, and soon it would be a big party. V would start having a white wine, saying he had to get going, but before long he was drinking peppermint schnapps and singing "Runaround Sue" with the jukebox, dancing on the table. He looked like he liked being with his players, and we were all having a good time. Of course the next day, Pam would give us hell for keeping her husband out all night, but it was a party after every win.

I remember one time we played in Vegas, and we were coming home on the plane. I fell asleep, and woke up because I heard some noise. I looked up, and down the aisle comes a conga line. I mean everybody: players, boosters, flight attendants, even a pilot. And at the front is V! I remember thinking, "Who the hell is flying this plane?" But we had fun, always had fun.

Jimmy became a good *X*s and *O*s coach when he went to N.C. State, but really what he did best with us was just motivate us, get us to play hard, and let us go play. That sounds easy, but it isn't always, and V had unusual ways to keep it loose. I remember one day we got to practice and we were all sick of looking at each other, just tired of it all. And all of a sudden V yells, "Everybody outside." We went outside and had a snowball fight, as a team.

I would be in one of those situations, looking at a conga line, throwing snowballs, while we were playing ourselves into a top 20 ranking, and I would think to myself, "This is why I came here."

Later, things got a little out of whack between Ruland and Jim and their relationship soured for a time. But as a guy who led Iona to two NCAA bids, had a very strong pro career, got his degree from Iona, and is now the successful head coach at his alma mater, Ruland looks back and says simply, "I wouldn't change a thing. It has all worked out great for me."

What Iona was able to achieve was astonishing. In five years, they had gone from struggling to beat non–Division I teams to beating Louisville in the 9:00 game in a sold-out Madison Garden, winning back-to-back conference championships, earning two NCAA bids, and posting back-to-back years of 23–6 and 29–5. Dave Brown was part of an NCAA bid during his senior year, while Vickers and Hamilton garnered two NCAA berths before their graduations. Jeff Ruland had already been a part of two NCAA teams, and he was back for a senior year that promised to be a great one, as Iona had just completed a strong recruiting year. The future looked rosy indeed.

It was a time for soul searching and reflection for another reason, however. As Petriccione points out, with all the notoriety and success of the Iona program, it was apparent that opportunities would be there for Jim to move on if he chose:

> After we lost to Georgetown [at the Providence Civic Center] in the NCAA tournament, V asked me to walk around Providence with him. That wasn't unusual after a loss; we would often just walk and talk and he would wind down after the game. But this night was different. We must have walked for about four and a half hours. I later would kid V that we could have walked all the way back to New Rochelle with all the walking we did. But he had a lot on his mind. Iona had been very good to him, and he really loved New York. He was the athletic director at Iona by this time too, and he enjoyed that also. But he knew some big jobs might come his way, and he wasn't sure what he should do.
>
> I knew he was smart; I knew he worked hard, and could be a fund-raiser; he was a personality, and could even be a good administrator if he wanted to follow that path.
>
> But I learned the guy could coach too. I was amazed at little things he would do during a game that were great examples of bench coaching. I remember one game against Fairfield; they had a great player named Joe DeSantis, who is now the head coach at Quinnipiac. Most of our game plan was to contain DeSantis. Fred Barakat, the Fairfield coach, who was a good friend of Jim's, took DeSantis out with about seven minutes to go just to get a quick breather. After about a minute, V saw DeSantis head to the scorer's table to check back in. We had the ball, and it was a close game—we were up by a point or two. This was before the shot clock. V leapt up and called for our delay game, just to keep DeSantis from getting back into the game! We were holding it and holding it, and the

clock was down to five minutes, four minutes, three minutes, and Barakat was yelling at V, "You SOB! I let you speak at my camp all summer and this is what you do, you %$#%@&!" And V yelled back, "The only reason you have 250 kids at your $%#&@ camp is because I speak there!" This is all while the game was going on!

Finally they had to foul just to get DeSantis back in. We had some very good free throw shooters. We made them all, and we wound up winning the game.

And the coaches' friendship wasn't destroyed; not even damaged. Jimmy later helped Fred become the supervisor of officials for the ACC, a job he did well, and he and Jim remained close friends until Jim's death.

Jim had achieved all his goals at Iona with one exception—winning a national championship. There were lots of things to keep him at Iona, not the least of which was a recently created, very generous five-year contract that he had just agreed to. And, like his players, Jim didn't feel his Iona team was far from contending for a national title. But something else was bothering him a great deal. In 1979–1980 the Big East was formed, and many of the Northeast's premier Catholic institutions—Georgetown, St. John's, Boston College, Villanova, Seton Hall— had joined. Iona was not included, nor were they likely to be. Jimmy felt that those teams were going to leave the rest behind in the quest for the national championship in that region of the country, and frankly, in the 20-plus years since, he's been proved correct.

Still, he liked Iona, loved Jeff Ruland, felt at home in New York, and had a good team for the next year. What to do? Rich Petriccione, Jim's former manager, but now an integral part of the Iona program, found himself in the unusual position of giving advice to a man 15 years his senior:

I said to Jim, as we walked and walked that night in Providence, that in all honesty I felt Iona was a place you *could* get to the NCAA tournament and, as we had just proved, could win a game. It was a place you could go maybe 2–1, 3–1, even 4–1 in the tournament. But really, not a place you could expect to go 6–0. There were only a very few of those types of programs in the country.

As I said earlier, it didn't matter who you were; if what you said made sense, V would listen and it would help shape his opinion. And, from that moment, he decided he wanted to try to be a part of a program where it was practical to think they could go 6–0 in the NCAA tournament. It was the most realistic way to pursue the ultimate dream—winning the national championship.

He always said that that talk was what convinced him, and in a way, I'm proud of that. That he would value my opinion so much, it not only helped make his mind up, but that he would tell people throughout his life that he was influenced by my thoughts. "Gotta get to a place where you can go 6–0 in the tournament, Pet," he would say.

And it wasn't long before he wound up at one. North Carolina State University.

──[PROFILE: RULES]──

YOU'VE HEARD OF THE JORDAN RULES, RIGHT? WELL LONG BEFORE MJ came along, Jim had his own version that in retrospect might have been known as the "Rules Rules." Rules as in Jeff Ruland, of course, one of the most influential figures in my brother's life. In his three years at Iona, he was dominant in every sense of the word. Jimmy coached his share of NBA players during his career, but he always said that without question the best player he ever coached was Jeff Ruland.

Not only was recruiting him a real coup that brought the Iona program national attention, it was also a key building block in a career that took him to North Carolina State and, eventually, a national championship. Whether he could have achieved as much as he did without Jeff Ruland is a question no one can answer. With his motivational skills and his ability to connect with people, he may have found another route to accomplish the things he did. But it's certainly fair to say that Ruland gave Jim's career a huge boost. I always felt that if Jim could get on a big stage, people would notice what I knew to be true—that this guy was funny, smart, talented, and a great coach. Without Ruland, Jim would not have gotten that national stage, at least not at that time. Rich Petriccione likes to kid that whenever something good happened in your life, Jim would always claim to be the cause of it. "You know why you're athletic director at Iona now, Pet?" Rich can hear Jim asking. "Because of me!" Nevertheless, Jim was smart enough to know that a coach is nothing without good players, and Rules was simply the best he ever coached.

They had a complicated relationship, less like a player and his coach and more like a simple friendship. And unfortunately they had a falling-out when Jim left Iona to go to N.C. State. One could argue that Jim should have known better; coaches in their thirties are not supposed to be "friends" with their teenage players; they are supposed to be teachers, mentors, and, if anything, father figures. But for better or worse, Jim did not have a problem being friends with many of his players, especially with Ruland.

Ruland was, and is, like Jim in many ways: street-smart with a tough exterior, but sensitive, bighearted, and loyal. Because of that, while Jim was friends with many of his players, his relationship with Ruland was different even by his own unique player-coach standards. They were like colleagues in many ways. Ruland was always playing pranks on Jim. He'd have him paged in airports whenever the team traveled: "Doctor Nose, Doctor Nose, would Doctor Nose please pick up the nearest white courtesy telephone?" He'd hide Jim's airline tickets and not tell him where they were until the very last minute, leaving Jim to make a mad dash to the airport. But they definitely clashed at times. After a 5–0 start during Ruland's freshman year, they suffered an embarrassing loss to Holy Cross and in the midst of all the finger-pointing and recriminations, Rules and Vickers threatened to quit the team. In the heat of the moment, Jim said fine, go ahead. It was only Anita Swanson, Ruland's mother, who saved the day and talked sense into both sides.

Calling their relationship unique is as much an understatement as calling Michael Jordan a pretty good basketball player. Because their friendship was so different, people have had a hard time understanding it. The common perception is that Ruland was mad at Jim for leaving him and taking the N.C. State job before his senior year. Ruland said in no uncertain terms that that's not true:

> I would gladly have gone to N.C. State with Jim. I had no problem with him taking that job. V told me Pam was pregnant again, and it was a great opportunity for him and his family, and it was. I never had a problem with that, and I told him that. The only problem I ever had was right after he took the job, he called me at my mom's house, and said something that I can only say really, really, hurt me. He basically knew what I was about then, and I still am today, and that's loyal. And he said something that implied somehow I wasn't loyal to him; I felt I could never forgive him for that.
>
> That is why we had the falling-out. It's that simple. It was that phone call, and it had nothing to do with his taking the N.C. State job.

Some additional background is necessary here, because that phone call was about more than just Jim taking the new job. Jim had had some business dealings with an agent, Paul Corvino, who had also illegally signed up Ruland before his senior year, costing him his last year of eligibility. The NCAA came in to investigate, and Iona was under siege. At a crucial time when he really needed his friend, mentor, and former coach, Ruland interpreted what Jim said during that phone call as, "Hey, get that situation straightened out so things don't get screwed up for *me!*" and based on that interpretation, it's hard to blame him for feeling betrayed and reacting the way he did.

Jim apparently did make several gestures toward reconciliation over the years, but frankly, if he had been serious about it, he would have been successful. He was the adult in the situation, or at least the authority figure, and could be very persuasive when he wanted to be. He always said that Ruland was going to have a great pro career and that after he had established himself, they would meet as equals, as two successful adults, and talk things out. In fact, such a meeting did take place when Ruland drove down to Raleigh in 1988 after his NBA career, but again, Jim's effort was only perfunctory, and he never brought the subject up. Ruland recalled the visit:

> We really didn't talk about what happened at Iona much. We had a nice visit, but I kept waiting for Jimmy to say something, to bring the subject up, and he never did. I was really disappointed by that. You know that [the phone call] was the only thing that kept us apart. I look back now, and life's too short, you know? I lost my mother, my father-in-law, and Jimmy's gone. I'm 42 years old. It's just silly—life's too short to hold grudges and to let silly things like that get between friends. I wish we could have mended those fences. We let that whole thing go on way too long, and unfortunately I can't change that now.

Jeff Ruland took Iona to the NCAA tournament in his second year as head coach, faster than any coach in the school's history. The night they won the MAAC tournament and got the NCAA bid, he joined me on ESPN Radio. I wasn't sure how he would react to my interviewing him on his very special night, and I certainly wasn't going to bring up my brother's name or their relationship. I was a bit apprehensive about the delicacy of the situation, but right at the start, completely unprompted, Ruland said, "I know Jimmy was watching down on us tonight. What a great night! Everything good that's happened to me is because I came to Iona in the first place, and I came here because of him. Jimmy, this one's for you!" He was crying tears of joy, and I could hardly speak. It was one of the most emotional moments I've ever shared, and the warmest and most thoughtful gesture he could have made.

Because it needs to be said, and because Jim can't say it, I'll say it for him: Jeff, I'm sorry you and Jim didn't mend the fences better. You were such an important person in his life and the life of his family that that is, and always will be, regrettable. You were bighearted enough to share your feelings with a national radio audience, and I want to honor the unique friendship you and Jimmy had, and try to rekindle it in some way. If Jim had heard your comments that night on the radio, whatever fences were broken would never have been left unmended—they would have been fixed or replaced altogether. Like you, Jeff, Jim had a soft side, a big heart, and there's no way he could have heard your comments and not been as moved as I was. On behalf of his family, I hope you'll let us call you a friend in the future, a friend that will spend time with us, join us in V Foundation events, and let us share in your talent and success—and maybe even drive a golf cart into the lake with you at Split Rock Golf Course!

8

RUN TO THE TITLE

CONTROVERSY SWIRLED AROUND JIM AFTER HE ACCEPTED THE NORTH Carolina State job. For the first few months, things were pretty bizarre. There would have been pressure enough *without* the Ruland situation, what with accepting a high-profile job at a big-time program and making a major family move. The ACC is an absolute hotbed of basketball fever; one of the reasons Bill Foster left Duke was that he found it difficult to make the adjustment to becoming such a public figure. He used to joke that as the coach of the Blue Devils, when you buy a carton of milk the morning paper has the story and the afternoon paper has pictures.

Jim found this out in a hurry when he was asked to sign autographs at a local shopping mall right after he took the job. "Why would anybody want your autograph?" asked his 11-year-old daughter Nicole. Jim's answer was revealing:

> The people are not excited about meeting *me*. They don't even know me. But what they love and respect is this position, this office, the *head basketball coach at North Carolina State*. It could be you, it could be Mom, it could be this plant . . . they just love N.C. State and they love its basketball team. So they want to meet me for that reason. It's pretty simple, but it's still pretty special.

There would have been the usual excitement and chaos that goes with any new job even without the added distraction of the situation that was developing at Iona. What was transpiring there *was* bizarre, and in many ways sad. Jim had flown to Raleigh after N.C. State's athletic director,

Willis Casey, had called to see if Jim had any interest in the head coaching job. He didn't wait for any details, didn't ask any questions about the terms of a potential contract; he just got on a plane and flew down immediately. His philosophy throughout his career had always been that the *second* contract you received was the most important one. If you proved that you could *do* the job at a certain place, you were in a stronger position and had a lot more to offer than just the prospect of what you could do there.

Even though he had just agreed to a generous, five-year deal with Iona, Jim accepted the N.C. State job shortly after the first interview. Here's his version of events:

> Willis Casey called me and said, "How would you like to come down here and be our next basketball coach?" I was stunned! It was all so fast! I stammered something out, like "Well, what about the contract? The salary? Talking to Pam, to my family, the people at Iona?" And Casey said, "What happened to the guy who just wanted the opportunity? I'm giving you the opportunity." I started begging for more time, and Casey said, "Jim, we're having a press conference at 2:00 P.M. tomorrow to introduce our new basketball coach. It's either going to be you or someone else who really wants the job. I need to know either way by 11:00 tonight." I didn't know the salary, the length of the contract, where we would live . . . nothing. Still, after spending the day talking with Pam and some other people close to me, I called Willis Casey at 11:00 P.M. and told him I accepted the job. It was only then that I found out what the salary was going to be [considerably less than he was making at Iona], and the length of the contract.

Once Jim agreed to take the job, Casey gave him an extra day to clear up business in New York before the press conference. Brother Driscoll became so upset when Jim told him that he was going to N.C. State that Driscoll had to ask Jim to leave so he could compose himself before continuing their discussion. Iona had been very generous to Jim, and Driscoll in particular was hurt and disappointed.

Jim and his top assistant, Pat Kennedy, had already agreed that they would strongly urge Driscoll to promote Kennedy to the head coaching position, arguing that the great recruits who had already committed would still come, and the program could continue uninterrupted. After some reflection, Driscoll understood why Jim wanted to go; however, despite this understanding, the chaos began almost immediately. Iona wanted to make the announcement that Jim was going to N.C. State and that Pat Kennedy would be taking over right away. Jim was horrified, since State had reluctantly delayed their own press conference, but still wanted to be the ones to announce their new head coach. Iona was insistent, Jim was angry, and Kennedy, whose support Jim was trying to enlist to delay the announcement, was caught in the middle. It caused a little rift in their relationship, since Jim wanted Kennedy's loyalty, while Kennedy (understandably) wanted to get off on the right foot with the people at Iona. So a silly compromise was reached: Iona announced that Jim was resigning and that Kennedy was taking over as coach, but no mention was made of where Jim was going.

Well, it wouldn't have taken a rocket scientist to figure out that this would please no one. Both sides were a little upset with Jim because of the way things had played out, but it seemed that everyone would be able to move past it, and things would be fine. At the press conference at State, Jim was funny and entertaining, and Driscoll finally gave him his blessing.

Then the you-know-what really hit the fan. It was revealed that Jeff Ruland had signed with an agent and would be ineligible for his senior year. Jim and Ruland had their own major falling-out. On top of that, one of the three great recruits who had signed with Iona decided to back out. Brother Driscoll got wind of what was going on, and he too became suspicious and angry. Had Jim bailed out because he knew in advance about Ruland's signing? Jim had had some business dealings with the agent Ruland had signed with. The NCAA began an investigation and Brother Driscoll stopped talking to Jim because of the perception of collusion.

Making matters worse was the fact that Jack Wilkenson, a reporter for the New York *Daily News*, had taken it upon himself to "expose" the Iona program. His stories were being splashed across the sports pages almost every day. Down at State, Casey was great about it. He was used to constant bombardment from the press about various aspects of ACC basketball, so he took most of the stories with a grain of salt and chalked them up to the Iona community's disappointment about Jim's departure. But as the allegations against Jim grew in scope and intensity, Casey too became concerned. Still, Jim always felt that Casey was very supportive during that difficult time.

And it was a pretty wild time. I was living in Hempstead, on Long Island, about 40 minutes from Manhattan; one night Jim called me at midnight. "Quick, I need you to drive into the city and get a paper as soon as they come off the press to see what the story is going to say about me tomorrow. I need to know what the allegations are going to be so I can be prepared." So, 2:00 in the morning, there I was driving to the *Daily News* printing plant, finding a guy loading a delivery truck with that day's papers, taking a copy back to Long Island, calling Jim an hour later. When I read him the story, he breathed a sigh of relief and relaxed because there wasn't really anything new.

Wild times indeed. But Jim weathered the storm and things got better. N.C. State was a great place to be and Jim fell in love with it quickly. One of the first things he told me after he got there was that the best point guard he had ever coached was in his program. His name was Sidney Lowe, and he was just a rising sophomore—although nowadays he's head coach for the Memphis Grizzlies. Remembered Lowe:

> One of the first things V told us when he came in was that he owed us nothing, and that we needed to understand that. What we were going to get we had to earn, so we needed to be ready to go play. It seemed kind of gruff at first, but it was a way of saying everybody had a clean slate with him. And it didn't take long until I began to feel like we were part of his family. He created that type of family atmosphere and it was obviously important to him. It was also obvious right away that he was going to create an atmosphere that was simple and straightforward with his players. Shooters shoot. Rebounders rebound. And the point guard runs the show. I was that point guard, so it was my job to run everything.

In Jim's first year, the Wolfpack had to go to Madison Square Garden and play in the Holiday Festival. As fate would have it, their first round matchup was against Iona College. It was, to say the least, a hostile crowd. People fired Christmas ornaments at Jim from the stands when he was introduced, and he was booed throughout the game. Iona was young and fired up; N.C. State was lucky to hang on and win, 61–58. They went on to beat perennial powerhouse St. John's in the final to win the championship, and Lowe was voted tournament MVP. Lowe again:

What set V apart was that he understood what you were capable of and simply asked you to do that, letting you know that he *believed* you could and would do it. Other coaches try to tell you what you can't do, and steer you away from those things. V did the opposite, encouraging us to do what we did well, and telling us that if each of us focused on those things, our team had no limits. It made us feel, as a group, there was nothing we couldn't accomplish.

My junior year there was still no shot clock, and especially late in games, I would have a lot of ball-handling responsibilities as we managed the clock. I was getting pretty tired in one game with about five minutes to go, and I gave V the fist sign, signaling that I wanted to come out for a rest. I thought I saw him look away, so I called over to him and put up the fist again. This time I was sure he saw me, and he just looked away. Now I was yelling at him, "Hey Coach, I need a blow . . ." and he was ignoring me. Finally there was a foul and I walked over to the bench and said, "Coach, didn't you hear me? I need one here . . . gimme a blow!" And V walked over and said, "Sidney, there will be plenty of time to rest later. I'm not taking you out until your eligibility runs out."

The Holiday Festival championship turned out to be one of the few highlights of the season as the Wolfpack went on to post a 14–13 record in Jim's first year. Despite the team's mediocre performance, the school, the fans, and the administration made Jim and his family feel welcome in North Carolina with their warm Southern hospitality. Jim was being asked to speak so often that he feared he was running out of material, so he came up with this story to add to his repertoire:

The fan mail that we coaches get here in the ACC is unbelievable. It is so intense down here. One letter writer sent me a note after we lost to arch-rival Carolina for the second time in a row. It said, "Coach, I know you're trying real hard and all, but I'm not sure you realize how we feel about losing to Carolina. That's twice now in the same season, and if it happens again, I'm going to come to Raleigh and shoot your dog." Now most notes like this in other places would be sent anonymously.

Not here. This note was signed and included a home phone number, return address, and a sheet of references! It was then that I began to appreciate how seriously they took this rivalry. So I wrote back and said that I didn't like losing to Carolina any more than he did, and I didn't plan on doing it too much longer. I ended it by saying, "P.S. I don't have a dog." About a week later a UPS truck came to our house and delivered a package. Inside was a little pooch who had a note around his neck that said, "Don't get too attached."

Sidney Lowe's backcourt mate was Dereck Whittenburg, who had played alongside him since their days at DeMatha High School under legendary coach Morgan Wooten. He remembers the first time he met Jim, back when he was still in high school and Jim was still at Iona:

Sidney and I were playing in the Boston Shootout our senior year. We both played well, and we won the championship. We both had already committed to N.C. State. After the championship game, V comes walking past us and just says, "I love you two #$@!!$%!! guards. You guys are great . . . just great!" And he walked away. Sid and I looked at each other and said, "Who the hell was that?" Two years later I wound up playing for him, and at least I knew *he* knew who *we* were when he said it, and must have liked what he saw in that Boston tournament. He had charisma right from the start, and he was easy for us to like. I felt close to him right away, but he was definitely different, no question about that.

Another of the trio of then-sophomore stars on that team, Thurl Bailey, also had a strong impression that his new coach would do things differently. But he didn't particularly like it at the time:

It was midway through my sophomore year, and I was definitely getting behind in my studies, largely because I wasn't going to class regularly. Coach V called me into his office one day and while we were talking about it he said casually, "I guess it doesn't bother you that you're an idiot."

I was puzzled at first. "What are you talking about?"

"I guess it doesn't bother you that people think that you're an idiot. It's the only thing I can assume."

Now I was furious! "People don't think I'm an idiot! Who feels like that? Do *you* think I'm an idiot?"

And V said, "I didn't say I thought you were an idiot. I said I guess it doesn't bother you that other people will think that. What else can they think? You're smart enough to do the work here, your education is being paid for, your books, your room, and you won't even go to class! People will say that is the behavior of an idiot, and since you won't even get your butt to class, I can only assume you don't mind that."

I was still furious. "I am not an idiot!" I knew what he was doing, but still it angered me enough that I did start going to class, got my grades up, and eventually got my degree. The spark for all of it, though, was that day that Coach V got me so mad.

In his second year at State, Jim became an outspoken advocate for the shot clock. "Ours is the only game around," he used to say, "where you can choose simply not to play. That's ridiculous." Yet since there *wasn't* a shot clock, and he had terrific guards who could handle the ball, shoot free throws, and not turn it over, he played ball control and held the basketball. A lot. People questioned him about this all the time; this is how he once responded at a press conference:

Human beings are marvelous creatures capable of doing many things, and some are even able to hold two thoughts simultaneously in their minds.

I would very much like to see a shot clock. I think it would be better for the game. But as you may have noticed, we are *not* using one at the present time, and I think my best chance to win—without the clock—is to play the way we are playing. Two different thoughts.

Typical games during that year were two losses (39–36 and 45–40) to Terry Holland's No. 1–ranked Virginia team, wins over Southern Miss (46–45), St. Peter's (44–43), and the kicker—in the ACC tournament—a win over Maryland 40–28! 40–28? What were they using, the two-handed set shot? It was bizarre. Yet that *was* the best way for his team to win without the shot clock. And win they did, going 22–10 and getting an NCAA bid but bowing out in the first round of the tourney to UT-Chattanooga, 58–51.

Things really looked bright for Jim's third year at N.C. State in the fall of 1982, that memorable season that would prove to be so special. It was special for me as well, not only to share in Jim's success but because it marked my first year as a college head coach. At 25, I was named head coach at Kutztown University, alma mater of football great Andre Reed, who was a student while I coached there, and was probably a good enough basketball player to play hoops there as well. They were coming off a rebuilding year, having won 10 games the year before, and had never won more than 15 games in their 50-year history. Still, I was excited about the opportunity.

I lost my first game on a buzzer beater in overtime. Then we lost again by three, won in overtime, then lost by two, four, two, and in overtime again. We were so close! Jim gave me a call and asked how our team was doing. I said, "Oh man, we've been so close! We're 1–6 but we lost twice in overtime, by two twice, by three once, by four . . ." Jim interrupted me. "Well, I know what your problem is," he said. I was eager to hear what he had to say next. "You suck. You've got a bad team. You're 1–6! What difference does it make: 2 points, 4 points, 24 points . . . you have one win. You have to do better." Like the advice he gave to Thurl Bailey, it wasn't especially pleasant, but it was good advice. And I never forgot it. If you ever try to be "just good enough," you never are. Close doesn't count. You have to be better.

His own team was definitely better. With a trio of outstanding seniors in Bailey, Lowe, and Whittenburg, and coming off an NCAA bid, things looked promising indeed. But after an encouraging 7–2 start, all the hopes for a great season crashed to the floor when Dereck Whittenburg broke his foot in an 88–80 loss to Virginia. The doctors said it was questionable whether he would return at all before the end of the season, but according to Whit, Coach Valvano had other plans:

> Immediately after the game where I got hurt, V was a mess. He was angry, frustrated, depressed, agitated. He kept saying, "I can't believe you're going to lose your senior year. It just isn't right." And it was obvious how much he hurt for me; he was really down.

The very next day I saw him again and he was completely different. He came to me all excited and said, "Whit, you're gonna come back from this! You are gonna get better and come back and play for us this year, your senior year! You are going to come back like Willis Reed and lead us to a championship!"

He was so adamant about it, I just said, "Well, OK . . . then I will." And really, from that day, I completely believed I would be back and play that year. Not a doubt in my mind. I believed it, because he believed it.

The reason for Jim's change in attitude was simple. That evening he had reread the words of one of his heroes, Vince Lombardi, who said, "A leader does not have the luxury of self-pity. He must be the first believer." From then on, he became just that. Because he believed, others did also.

Whit was able to come back, against Virginia, some 14 games later. But by then, N.C. State was facing the very real possibility of not even making the NCAA tournament. Their record stood at 16–8 with only two games left.

Worse for Jim, he had a difficult decision to make. Ernie Myers, a freshman, had stepped in and played brilliantly in place of Whittenburg, and the team, after a period of adjustment, had responded by winning seven of their last eight games, including the last three in a row. What to do now that Whit was ready to step back in? Jim felt the right thing to do was to go with Whit, the senior, since it was his last chance, while Myers had three more years. The team lost its last two games to wind up at 16–10, and it did not look good. Can you say, "N.I.T.?"

However, this was a season of miracles. The team received its first of several when they won the ACC tournament in heart-stopping fashion—a one-point win over Wake Forest (71–70), an overtime win over North Carolina (91–84), and then a win over Ralph Sampson and Virginia (81–78) for the ACC championship. Said Whittenburg:

> Since we weren't really sure we were even going to make the NCAA tournament, every game was so big for us, and then the *way* we would win them! I mean we steal the ball in the last half minute to win the game against Wake, we come back from the dead in regulation to force overtime and then beat Carolina, and then make another comeback to win over

Virginia. Between those comebacks and my own comeback, I was so excited just to know that I was going to get to keep playing, that at the end of the games I would go to V and just pick him up! Find him, grab him, and celebrate! We're going to play again!

N.C. State got their invitation to the dance. But Jim was none too thrilled with Pepperdine, his first-round opponent, coached by Jim Harrick. V actually told Frank Dascenzo of the *Durham Sun* that if N.C. State could get out of the first round, he thought they'd win the whole tournament. Think about the paradox of that statement! Here's a guy who thinks his team is good enough to win the national title, but isn't sure if he can beat Pepperdine in the first round! It meant he knew just how good they could be; the statement proved to be prophetic.

With State trailing by six points with only 70 seconds to play in overtime, the Pepperdine game looked to be over. This, remember, was before the shot clock and the three-point basket. Things got even bleaker when, 25 seconds later, Lowe fouled out of the game with State still down by four. At the line was Dane Suttle, a terrific player and an 84 percent free throw shooter. However, most of the fans had already given up. The Pepperdine players were celebrating on the bench, and who could blame them? It was over . . . except that it wasn't over. Suttle missed and State scored to pull within two, and then quickly fouled Suttle again. He missed again! With nine seconds left, Pepperdine fouled Whittenburg, who had a one and one for a chance to tie. Jimmy put in Cozell McQueen.

It's funny, looking back on a championship run, how the smallest of details can decide the outcome. That goes a long way toward explaining a coach's paranoia. This small, seemingly insignificant decision, as much as anything, made the national championship possible. McQueen was in for one reason: in case Whit missed, he was to tap back the rebound and hope for another try. He was all arms and legs. Sure enough, Whit did miss. But McQueen didn't tap it—he caught it! And went up himself, an awkward, off-balance shot that somehow went in! Tie game! Pepperdine rushed it up, threw up a desperation try, and was now faced with double overtime. State had had Lowe foul out, was forced to foul the Waves' best player and free throw shooter *twice*, missed their own opportunity at the line—and still found a way to tie the game. Think Pepperdine's players might have been a bit shell-shocked?

Jimmy always said that while most people say the "Team of Destiny" run to the NCAA title started in the ACC tournament, he always felt it started with that game against Pepperdine.

The remainder of the run through the NCAA tournament has been well documented in other places; the thing that was truly amazing was the caliber of the teams State had to beat. Keeping in mind that they had to get past North Carolina and Virginia—two teams ranked in the top three in the nation at some point—just to win the ACC and get invited to the NCAA tournament, the road to the Final Four was nothing short of astonishing in its difficulty. After Pepperdine, they had to face UNLV, a team that was also ranked among the top five in the nation during the season; Utah in Utah, basically a road game in the NCAA tournament; then Virginia again, who were ranked No. 4 in the nation at that point. Whittenburg and his sharpshooting teammates shot 28 of 41 against Utah, which provided a comfortable win sandwiched between two one-point victories (71–70 over UNLV and 63–62 over Virginia in Ralph Sampson's last collegiate game).

That Virginia game was one for the books. It was unbelievably tense. Virginia had the ball, down by one point, with a chance for one last shot and the win. They missed, got their own rebound, the ball went up again, and they miss again! The game is over! We win!

So now it was destination: Albuquerque. State had won eight in a row and was definitely hot. Georgia, their semifinal opponent, like the other two regional champs—Louisville and Houston—and unlike State, had received a first-round bye. They had just come off back-to-back wins over St. John's and North Carolina. They had a good team, but State raced out to a huge lead and held on to win despite sputtering late in a much slower game than the other semifinal, in which Houston upended Louisville in a "dunkfest." It was on to the championship for Houston and State.

Sidney Lowe remembers the championship game:

> V's pregame talk was pretty short actually, but he did some great things in it. It wasn't a lot of *X*s and *O*s . . . the best thing he did was simply remind us of one thing: we *deserved* to be there. We were a good team, a good team playing well, and had made the plays that earned our way there. We had made those plays against some of the best teams and against some of the best players in the country. We deserved to be there. When I

went out for introductions, I just kept smiling and laughing to myself. After the game, people asked me what I was laughing at. I just told them I was remembering what V had said in the locker room. It all hit me. We did deserve to be there, and it all felt good, real good.

I had a good idea how State would approach the game, since Jim, myself, and assistant coach Tom Abatemarco had discussed it the previous evening over a cup of coffee. I asked him point blank if what everyone was saying was true: that State had little or no chance. I also asked about what he himself had been saying publicly: that if State won the opening tip, they might not take a shot until Tuesday morning. He said, "I don't know if we'll win, but there is no way they are going to blow us out. Our guards are too good to let that happen. It will be close." As far as slowing the pace and holding the ball, he gave me good advice, which I used in my own coaching career and still use in analyzing games today. Usually, he said, the underdog can't pull an upset by holding the ball the whole game; they can keep the score close that way, but they ultimately end up losing. So, he contended, upset games frequently followed a pattern of run-hold-run. The underdog had to come out aggressive and establish that they could play with the favorite, and ideally take the lead early if possible. The favorite would then regroup and the underdog would have to fight them off for a while. What that would do is what State had done throughout the tournament: keep the other team off balance and put State in a posi- tion to win down the stretch with another late run.

I think Jim felt confident that with Lowe, Whittenburg, and another guard who was playing well then, Terry Gannon, State would be able to attack early and have enough counterpunches in the middle to stay close. The problem would be making that last run at the end. Could they make the plays late in the game? You can never know that for sure, but Jim felt that, as great as Houston was, his team would be in that position.

While not every upset follows this pattern, for the Houston game it was like a script. N.C. State came out and took 18 shots in the first five minutes, to Houston's six. Even though I had sat with Jim the night before and knew he wanted to attack, I was taken aback. I knew that if they kept that pace up, N.C. State wouldn't have a chance.

Of course, they *couldn't* keep up that pace. The game followed Jim's prediction: State ran early, then settled in and played an almost perfect half

My two older brothers, Nick (age seven) and Jim (age three), lifelong Yankee fans.

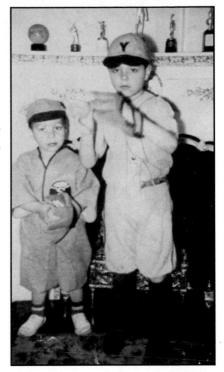

Jim at Seaford High School, an all-star in three sports.

Jim's biggest thrill: playing in Madison Square Garden.

The Rutgers 1966–1967 basketball team, which finished 22–7, third in the NIT. Jim and Bob Lloyd, cocaptains, are touching the basketball.

Jim with two of Iona's best, Glenn Vickers and Jeff Ruland.

Jim coaching at Iona College in New Rochelle, New York. Next to him are Pat Kennedy and Rich Petriccione. Jim was fond of introducing himself by saying, "Hi, I'm Jim Valvano. Iona College."

According to Jim, "the real coach in the family," our dad, Rocco.

Jim and me with our mom.

Jim and Pam with the girls on vacation at the beach.

Jim with our mom and dad and his daughter, Nicole, on vacation in Greece.

Jim cutting down the net after the Wolfpack beat Virginia 81–78 for the ACC Championship, March 13, 1983. Photo courtesy of AP/Wide World Photos.

Holding the trophy up over the crowd during the victory celebration after the biggest win of his career, 54–52 over Houston at the Pit in Albuquerque, April 5, 1983. Photo courtesy of AP/Wide World Photos.

The infamous boat painting (see page 133).

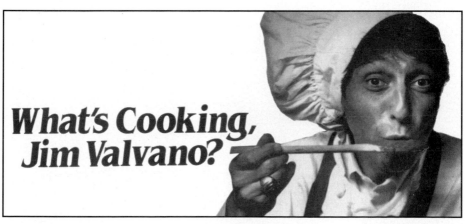

A publicity picture promoting Jim Valvano's Guide to Great Eating.

Talkin' hoops with John Saunders on ESPN.

Veteran Brent Musberger with the new rookie on ABC.

to lead by eight at the intermission (33–25). They scored their first basket on a dunk, and got four fouls on Clyde Drexler. Houston was slowed down tremendously.

Then, as Jim himself later said, he got greedy. His philosophy, which had been refined and repeated through the years, and which had served him so well in the postseason, was simply "survive and advance." Don't think about winning six games in the postseason; in fact, don't even think about winning the whole thing at all. Don't worry about the next game, tomorrow, next week. Win this game right now! Win this half right now! Win this possession—right now! Do whatever you have to do to survive, advance, and play again. But now for the first time, this close to the whole prize, he challenged the players to focus on it. He told them that to come this close, to lead by eight at the half, to have 20 minutes separating them from the championship, and then to let it slip away would haunt them for the rest of their lives.

Perhaps the enormity of it all began to sink in. Perhaps the unfamiliarity of playing with the lead was a factor. Definitely Houston was too good not to make some sort of a run. In any case, whether the cause was Jim's "greed" or some other factor, it is difficult to imagine a more dismal start to a half of basketball than State endured during the first 10 minutes of the second half. They were outscored 17–2, and found themselves down 42–35.

Remembered Lowe:

> We didn't have a sinking feeling at that point; it was more anger, really, that we had let them do that to us. We had been down so many times before though, that it worked in our favor then, because we certainly weren't going to give up. We just tried to make some plays, create some turnovers, and see what would happen.

What happened, among other things, is that Sidney continued his masterful performance. He played all 40 minutes, had eight points and eight assists, made five steals, and did not have a single turnover. Houston coach Guy Lewis went into a delay game, which most people vehemently criticized. However, Jim himself told me that this strategy had been successful for Houston throughout the year. There is an old saying in sports: "Ya gotta dance with the girl that brung ya," and this strategy was a part of

what brought Houston to the Final Four. But on that night, it was inef-
fective—partly because N.C. State forced turnovers, but more because
Houston was not a great free throw shooting team and missed some coming down the stretch.

In fact, those were the only two statistical categories that State won in
the game; they made 6 turnovers to Houston's 13, and shot .727 from the
line (8–11) compared to .526 for Houston (10–19). Houston out-
rebounded them 44–34, had eight blocked shots (seven by Hakeem
Olajuwon) to State's two, and the shooting percentages were about even,
39 percent for State and 38 percent for Houston. State made six of their
last seven shots; with Whittenburg, Lowe, and Gannon shooting confi-
dently from the perimeter, it kept the defense honest enough to give Thurl
Bailey room on the baseline. He was the game's leading scorer, with 15.

When Lorenzo Charles' dunk with seconds left sealed the 54–52 victory, pandemonium erupted. Jim has told the story of running out onto the
court so many times that it remains, after his ESPY speech, the one that
people still refer to the most. Here it is in his own words:

> There I was out there searching for someone to hug. People
> were running every which way, everybody was hugging some-
> body, I knew the TV cameras were on me, and yet I could not
> find one person to hug! Where was I running? I was looking
> for Dereck because I had dreamed of this moment all my life
> and I knew that 60 million people were watching and I had
> been hugging Whit after all our games because he was my des-
> ignated hugger.
>
> I thought I would be making history here, because every
> weekend of my life I had watched *Wide World of Sports* and
> heard about the "thrill of victory and the agony of defeat," and
> watched that skier fall down and fly off the side of the ski jump
> ramp, while some poor woman in France is going, "Look,
> Pierre, here comes *ton pere!*" I felt as if all they ever showed was
> "the agony of defeat" and now I, Jim Valvano, was going to give
> them "the thrill of victory."
>
> I imagined the cameras would be zeroing in on me running
> in "slo-mo," and the crowd would be roaring, and I would be
> running, and Whit would be running, and "Chariots of Fire"
> would be playing in the background. It was going to be history!

Me! Whit! Slo-mo! Thrill of victory! History! Together! Hug! "Chariots of Fire"! And I'd be on TV forever.

Then I got to the middle of court, and there was no Whit. He was hugging somebody else! So I ran to the left, looking for somebody to hug. Everybody was already taken. I ran right, looking. Everybody was hugging. There was nobody left to hug! I had just won the national championship, I'm the 28th guy to do it, 60 million watching, and I had nobody to hug. Finally I found my athletic director, Willis Casey, my boss, and he gave me my big break, a very nice man. He grabbed me, he hugged me! Wonderful! Great, finally a hug! He wasn't Whit, but a hug's a hug. Slo-mo, "Chariots of Fire" hug.

And then Willis Casey kissed me, squarely on the mouth!

Sixty million people have now watched me running like a maniac, and then I fell into the arms of a 65-year-old man who kissed me on the mouth. The guy watching in Dubuque must have thrown down his beer and said, "Mabel, come look at this."

I felt the thrill of victory and the agony of defeat all at the same time.

That may be true, but if so, the thrill of victory was definitely paramount. Jim had been given a 10-year contract extension earlier in the year, even before the exciting postseason run, and the public and media seemed to be embracing him. Thad Mumau in the *Fayetteville Observer-Times* wrote, "I doubt the media has enjoyed anything as much as following this State team. Valvano is a trip in himself, and the whole team is not only a joy to witness, but a pleasure to be around." Echoed Mike Downey, "Valvano is an electric personality who encourages his players to be themselves, unlike those who believe basketball is more efficient when engineered by robotics."

It was a magical time. People not only appreciated what N.C. State was doing, but how they—and their coach—were doing it. With the new contract and the championship, the future could not possibly have looked any brighter. The storm clouds that were later to form on the horizon were nowhere to be seen.

9

Seashells and Balloons

One of Al McGuire's favorite phrases for describing good times was, "It was seashells and balloons." That certainly described Jim's tenure at N.C. State, at least until his last few years. After winning the championship in 1983 and an NIT bid the following year, State garnered NCAA bids in every year between 1985 and 1989. They reached the Elite Eight in two of those seasons, 1985 and 1986, won the ACC tournament in 1987, and were regular-season champions in both 1988 and 1989. Jim was also the ACC Coach of the Year twice during that stretch. As Casey Stengel says, "You can look it up."

Since so much has already been said about those achievements, this chapter won't spend much time dwelling on them, but will rather recount some of the "seashells and balloons" memories in the words of those who knew Jim best.

Here's one such story from Rich Petriccione:

> After Pat Kennedy and I had left Iona for Florida State, we were all in New Jersey for a summer camp there. It's Pat and me and Jim and his staff. The games start at 1:00, and Pat and I are in a new job and we are ready, pads and clipboards in hand, to find some players.
>
> By about 1:15, V is already bored, so he starts in. "You know what we need to do today?" he says. "We need to go bowling. Hey Pet . . . you ever been bowling?"
>
> I said, "One time in my life, like in sixth grade."
>
> "Well, today is a great day to go bowling," V says. "We gotta go bowling."

And I think, "Oh, geez, that's it . . . I know where this day is headed. It's gonna be three o'clock in the morning. I've seen this movie—hell, I've been *in* this movie with V many times before."

But we *have* to go bowling. And there we are, the coaching staffs of Florida State and N.C. State, in a bowling alley in New Jersey with V talking the whole time. "Hey Pet, you're really bad! You suck at bowling! I'm the best bowler here . . . none of you guys can bowl."

And I say, "V, I told you I only bowled once before!"

"Still," he says, "you are *really* bad." And we were pretty bad, but we spent the whole afternoon laughing our butts off.

Then we go to eat dinner. Next, we have more than a few beers. Sure enough, it's now like midnight, and we're not done yet. We go to the Princeton diner, right near the basketball camp, and now we've attracted some other coaches. Gary Williams has joined us, so now we have three big-time head coaches sitting at the same table, and I remember looking around the restaurant, thinking everyone was staring at us and thinking the same thing: I wanna be sitting with *them*. I gotta admit, as a young assistant coach, it felt pretty good to know everyone else in the diner wanted to be sitting where I was sitting.

V was in his "peach schnapps" phase. All of V's friends know the "peach schnapps" phase. *Everyone* had to have peach schnapps. And we've had more than a few. Everyone has now ordered a little breakfast, as it's about 2:00 A.M., and there's a half of an English muffin on the table. It's been sitting there for a while, and it's just soaked in butter. V turns to me and says, "Pet, you want that muffin?"

"No, V."

He turns to Kennedy. "Pat, you want it?"

"No V, I'm good."

"Gary, you?"

"No thanks, Jimmy . . ." And so it goes till everyone has turned the muffin down.

So V takes the English muffin and *slaps it into his forehead.* It has so much butter on it, it just sticks there. And V just continues on with his conversation as if nothing has happened, and now the butter is just dripping down his face, and running off his chin.

Finally, after several minutes with it there, he's talking with Pat, and the muffin falls back on the table. V says, "Pat, did you know I had an English muffin on my head?"

"Yeah, V, I saw the muffin there."

"And you didn't say anything? What kind of friends are these? I'm in a public diner with an English muffin stuck to my forehead, *and nobody says anything to me about it?*" By this point everybody was hysterical, including the diners at the surrounding tables, who couldn't help noticing that Jim Valvano was in their diner—with an English muffin stuck to his forehead.

Finally, as the perfect ending to this bizarre day, we go back to the hotel, and there's a big fountain in the lobby with fish in it. It's now about 3:30 in the morning. We're all about ready to drop, and just looking to get up to our rooms. Not V though. Still time for more. I look over at him and he's looking into the fountain. "V, what are you doing?"

"Gotta catch a fish before bed, Pet," he says. "Gotta do it like our ancestors . . . just climb in and get 'em with your bare hands." And sure enough, there he is, in his clothes and shoes, ankle deep in the fountain, then on his hands and knees, chasing after the fish, mumbling under his breath the whole time, "Come here, fish . . . just like our ancestors . . . bare-handed . . . don't need a fishing rod."

Needless to say, he's not having much success when finally the manager comes over and says, very nicely, "Coach, you're going to have to get out of the fountain now."

Jimmy says, "OK, but only if I can do somersaults all the way to my room." So he gets out of the fountain and starts doing somersaults across the lobby to the elevator. He gets to the elevator, presses the button *with his foot*, waits as the doors open, somersaults in, and the doors close to a standing ovation from the crowd!

Needless to say, in my 20-plus years in athletic administration and coaching, I haven't had too many days as unusual as that one, or as much fun, for that matter.

Broadcaster Bob Costas had another Valvano tale to tell:

When I had Jim on my radio show, we often would do the
show in a restaurant or some other public setting. And people
would just leave their dinners on the table and let them get
cold, they were so busy laughing at Jim. We decided to ask him
to guest host the program for me on occasion. As such, I got
to know him pretty well.

One of the first common threads for us was our childhood
love of Mickey Mantle. He'd heard that I carried a baseball
card of Mantle in my wallet, and I showed it to him. He told
me of the arguments he'd have with his father about
DiMaggio/Mantle, as so many sons and fathers probably had.
And he told me he had never met Mickey.

Well, I was to receive the Sportscaster of the Year award,
and as the recipient, you can select who you want to present
you the award. I asked Mickey Mantle if he would do it, and
he agreed. I called Jim and told him the news, and then asked
him if he would like to come to the banquet, where I would
introduce him to Mantle.

He was thrilled! He said, "Man, if Bob Schweiger only
knew . . . I'm going to meet Mickey Mantle!" I asked who Bob
Schweiger was and Jim said, "He was my best friend in high
school and he knew how much I loved Mickey. Wait until Bob
Schweiger hears about this!"

The night of the banquet, Jim typically starts in as soon as
he arrives. "When can I meet Mickey?" he says. I told him,
they were just starting dinner, let's wait a bit. Five minutes later
he's asking me again, pestering me throughout the evening like
a little brother. "Now? Can we go now?" Finally, dessert is over,
and I take Jim up to the dais to meet Mickey. He's chattering
the whole way. "I can't believe it! Mickey Mantle! Wait until
Bob Schweiger hears!"

We get to the podium, and I introduce Jim to Mickey, and
Mantle starts to climb laboriously out of his seat, awkwardly,
as his legs were very bad at this time. He struggles to his feet
and sticks out his hand to Jim. Jim shakes hands with Mickey,
looks him in the eye, and says, "Bob Schweiger says hello."
Mantle looks at me, perplexed, like, "Who *is* this guy?"

After the banquet many of the celebrities were socializing, and as is often the case at these kinds of events where people don't know each other that well, the conversation was subdued, polite, and mainly exchanges of pleasantries. Jim is starting to feel comfortable with all the folks, a number of whom he hadn't met before, and so he starts doing his shtick, and soon he has the room rolling with laughter, including Mantle, which doesn't go unnoticed by Jimmy.

The next day, as part of the awards weekend, I organized a celebrity baseball game against a local college for charity. We had Robert Klein, Joe Piscopo, Michael Weissman, some ex-major leaguers like Jim Kaat, and many others. Jimmy played shortstop, and Mickey, whose legs really wouldn't even allow him to swing anymore, managed our team in his full Yankee uniform.

Before the game, Jim and I approach Mantle in the dugout, and Jimmy drops to his knees, bowing, and says, "I have met my master!" Mickey is laughing, and Jimmy starts again like the night before . . . stories, one-liners. He has Mantle laughing so hard he has tears in his eyes.

Finally, Jimmy leaves to go out to the field, and Mantle just turns to me and says, "Damn, that is one funny son of a bitch." Perfectly Mantle, and when I shared that story with Jim later, I don't know if he ever looked more excited.

While my brother loved Mantle, it was Joe D who was my father's hero. My dad was a locally known sports personality in his own right, and through his own and later Jim's notoriety, he was able to meet many famous sports figures in his day. But one that he had never met was the Yankee Clipper.

In 1985, N.C. State faced St. John's in the NCAA regional final in Denver. My mother was in North Carolina watching her grandchildren while Pam went to the regional, and my father stayed in New York. When St. John's won to go to the Final Four, my mother flew back to New York, and my dad picked her up at LaGuardia Airport. While they were waiting for her luggage, who should also be waiting by the carousel but Joe DiMaggio! He says to my mom, "I have to go introduce myself and say hello. I'll be right back." He went over to Joe, and as my mother told the story many times later, Joe was very gracious and pleasant. Dad told him that he had played center field in his playing days because of his admiration for the way he, Joe, had played the game, and he boasted about his son Jim. DiMag was great about it all, and my mother said Dad came back looking like a kid again, he was so happy.

They got their bags, drove home, unloaded the luggage, and as my mother was putting some things away, my dad said he was going downstairs to take a nap. She heard a loud noise, and when she ran to see what it was, she found him collapsed at the bottom of the stairs. He was dead, instantly, as we were told later, of a massive heart attack.

About a year later, Jim was playing in the Crosby Invitational Golf Tournament in North Carolina. The evening before the event there was a big buffet, and as he was standing in line, who should be standing right behind him but Joe DiMaggio! Jim, startled, delighted, and awed all in a moment, turned to say something to him just as DiMag was having one of those "buffet moments": trying to balance his salad, his dinner plate, a roll, and his drink, all at the same time. Thinking quickly and realizing he didn't have a lot of time to strike up a leisurely conversation, Jim said, "Mr. DiMaggio, I'm Jim Valvano, the basketball coach at N.C. State. Joe made a move as if to try to shake hands, but he really couldn't, as he was loaded down with food. Jim made a gesture to forestall him and said, "I just wanted to tell you my father always admired you, you were his idol. He met you last year, and then he died."

DiMaggio's look turned to alarm. Had this crazed man come to somehow avenge his father's death? With a nod and a puzzled smile, DiMaggio made his way back to his table. Jim dazedly took his dinner back to his table, and as he slowly sat down Pam said, "You look pale as a ghost. What happened?"

Jim said, "I'm not sure, but I think I just told Joe DiMaggio that he killed my old man."

/ / /

Clay Moser was, as he puts it, "the lowest man on the N.C. State coaching totem pole" when he was beginning his career in basketball, a career that would eventually lead to administrative positions in professional basketball. Here's one of his classic stories about Jim:

> Jim had an idiosyncrasy where at halftime, he would basically chase the players into the locker room immediately after leaving the court. He'd make a point or two, or in some cases vent

his anger, then come out and talk to the assistants in the hall-way. After that meeting we would all go back into the locker room and, with a cooler head, Jim would make the adjustments he felt were needed. The assistants usually didn't go in for that first brief session; we just waited in the hall for Jim to come out.

In Hawaii in 1987, we had beaten Creighton and Louisville, and were now in the championship game against Arizona State. We had just played a miserable first half and were down by dou-ble digits at the break. Jim chases the team into the locker room and really reads them the riot act. We were just terrible, and he lets them know it. He comes back out into the hall, but he's really worked up this time. He is so ticked off, he can't even talk to us, and he turns to head back into the locker room again.

Dr. Jim Manley was the team doctor. He was loved and respected, and very loyal to N.C. State for many, many years. He was in his early to mid seventies at this point, with a small, somewhat fragile physique. The locker room had a swinging door separating it from the hallway, and Dr. Manley had walked in front of it after Jim left, not expecting him back for a few minutes. Suddenly, *wham!* Jim storms back into the locker room, sending Dr. Manley sprawling. He had been hit so hard, he slid clear across the floor and was now lying, half in, half out of a toilet stall on the other side of the room! Jim raced over to him, slid on his stomach under the stall, and held him in his arms, saying, "Doc, Doc. I'm so sorry. Are you OK?"

Well, the doctor had gotten absolutely blasted. The kids saw it all, and as much as they loved Dr. Manley, it *was* funny, and they were starting to laugh. Now Jim's getting angry at that as well. The training staff is there with the other team's doctor, all huddled around this stall with two men lying half inside, half outside, Jim refusing to leave Doc's side, when the buzzer sounds to signal the start of the second half! We haven't made any adjustments, haven't talked about anything. All Jim did was spend the whole intermission cradling Dr. Manley in his arms. Finally, Jim is convinced to head out to the court, leav-ing Doc in the hands of the medical staff.

Well, we go out and just dominate the second half. Outscore them by some 20-odd points and win by double digits. The players receive their awards, Charles Shackleford is named MVP, and about 20 minutes after game's end, we finally make it back to the locker room. As we open the door, who is standing there to greet us, as was his usual custom, but Dr. Manley!

The team files in and gets settled, and Jim says, "Great job, fellas!" Then he walks over to Dr. Manley, proceeds to put him in a headlock, and says, "If I have to kick the crap out of Dr. Manley at halftime of every game to get us to play like that, I'll do it, men!"

Doc, still in the headlock, chimed in with, "Whatever it takes, Jimmy, whatever it takes." It was a great and memorable incident, especially since Doc wasn't hurt seriously, and the team used it as a rallying cry the rest of the year, with Jim often saying, if the team was playing badly, "I'm gonna have to beat the crap out of Doc again."

Another time we were playing at the University of Virginia in a nationally televised afternoon game. In the locker room, Jim slipped on a wet floor and ripped his pants, not the first time that had happened to him. I had heard stories about him doing this before where he had to basically hold his pants together with his hands for the whole second half. Less than a minute later we hear the buzzer announcing the game about to start.

Evidently the stories were true, because as soon as Jim ripped his pants that day at UVA, without a word Dr. Manley went to his medical kit, took out a needle and thread, and started sewing. But the odd thing is that Jim doesn't even bother to take his pants off. They had apparently done the drill enough times before that Doc knew to just sew them while they were hanging down around his ankles.

So now Jim is barking out instructions to his assistants as they head out to the bench, and Doc is crouching behind him, sewing away, when Jim himself starts waddling out of the locker room and into the tunnel. "We open in a box and one on Stith . . ." he tells assistant Dick Stewart, still with his pants around his ankles, with Dr. Manley, duckwalking behind him, sewing all the way.

He has now followed Stewart so far out that they're almost to the opening to the arena. In fact, some UVA fans look into the tunnel and spot the N.C. State coach, pants around his ankles, with a squatting, sewing doctor in tow, yelling instructions on how to defend Bryant Stith, oblivious to the absurdity of the situation. V and Dr. Manley aren't able to finish the repair job until a few minutes into the game.

Jim sheepishly makes his way to the bench, sits down and says, "How we doin'?" Stewart points to the scoreboard, which showed us up 12–0. We won pretty easily, Dr. Manley's stitch job held up all day, and a small group of fans, it's safe to say, saw an ACC coach in a way they probably hadn't seen before, nor will be likely to again.

As anyone who has coached can tell you, the game itself can be so consuming that, like Jim at UVA, you can become oblivious to most outside things. Dereck Whittenburg recalls one such incident that took place after he joined the N.C. State coaching staff:

Late in games V did a good job shuffling players in and out . . . situation substitutions. We had a player from Greece, Panos Fasoulas, who was a very good defensive center for us. Late in games, if we had a lead, Jim would be sure to put Fasoulas in for defense.

We were playing in the Maui Classic. It was a talented team: Nate McMillan, Chris Washburn, Charles Shackleford. We're playing a good UNLV team. We get the lead late in what has been a close game. We make a turnover and V, who has been crouching in front of the bench, bolts to his feet, and just as suddenly, *bang*! He goes down, collapses right in front of the bench! People rush over to him, and I'm literally starting to cry. I think he's had a heart attack and he's dead.

Slowly, though, V starts coming to, but now the doctors are trying to hustle him off. No one knows what it is, and they want to check him out. Is it a heart attack? An aneurysm? I see Jim struggling to talk and all sorts of things are going through my mind. Is he asking us to save him, to help him? Can he tell us what's wrong? Are they some dying last words?

I lean in close to hear what V is saying, and he says, "Whit! Whit!"

"What, V, what is it? Tell me."

"It's their ball," he says. "Put Fasoulas in the game."

This seeming brush with death, which turned out to be nothing more than a harmless blood-pressure surge, perfectly illustrates Jim's dedication to the game.

The relationship between the media and coaches has always been complex, but perhaps never as adversarial as it is now. Jim, though, was either idealistic or naïve (or maybe he was even right): he felt that there was no reason why coaches and members of the media couldn't be friends. Said John Feinstein on the subject:

> One time I accompanied N.C. State to Hawaii. One night while we were there, Jim and Pam, my wife Mary and I, and a third couple were out at a little place that had a jukebox. Jim looked in and it was all filled with fifties and sixties songs. "Pammy!" Jim says, "These are the songs we grew up with. We've got to dance." Pam didn't enjoy dancing as much as Jim, but she does dance, and they're out there having a good time. That isn't enough for Jim. "C'mon," he says to the rest of us, "these are songs you *gotta* dance to. Get out here." And we did, so the six of us are out there dancing, having a good time.
>
> Finally, Pam wants to sit. That's fine. Jim dances with the other wives. They get tired . . . now none of the women want to dance anymore. Jim doesn't care. He stays out there and dances with David! We're finally ready to leave, and as we go, a song Jim really likes comes on. He starts dancing in the lobby as we're leaving.
>
> He just had to have fun, and while that's true of many people, what made him special is that he insisted—*demanded* even—that you have fun too! And he would often be the one to provide that fun if there were no other way.

Jim loved to dance. Once my brother Nick and his wife Karen, Jim and Pam, and my wife Darlene and I were in Manhattan having dinner— a great, wonderful dinner at a little upscale Italian place Nick went to regularly. When it ended, we were walking on a picturesque, tree-lined street on the Upper East Side past old brownstones with front stoops leading up to their doors. It had been raining earlier, so some of us had umbrellas, and suddenly Jim grabbed one and said, "You know, this looks like a movie set. I could see Gene Kelly dancing on this street." And with that, he starts doing just that: going up and down the steps of the various brownstones, doing an improvised dance number with an umbrella, much as he imagined Gene Kelly might. Up one stoop, down the next, now swinging around the pole of a street sign up and over a fire hydrant. It was funny and sweet and entertaining. While it may have lacked a bit of the panache of Mr. Kelly, it was no less inspired.

Again, John Feinstein describes Jim's fun-loving style:

> I can't say Jim "changed" my life, but there was a long time when he was a great presence in it. My philosophy has always been to stay around people smarter than you. When you leave them, you'll be smarter too. My mother was like that, and so was Jim, and I would often talk to both of them about things they had little direct knowledge of, because they had great instincts. Jim too, was a quick study, and to say he was a voracious reader is an understatement. He was always reading, and like everything else, he did that quickly too.
>
> I remember sending him my new book at the time, *A Season Inside*, about college basketball, in which Jim was one of the many college coaches with a prominent presence. I sent it to him on a Tuesday. Thursday morning he calls me and says, "John, I read your book. I really liked the part where you mention this and that . . ." and it was obvious he really had read it. Not just the parts where he was mentioned, but the whole book. In a day. He did that all the time.
>
> Of course, I used to say he had an unfair advantage. He only slept about an hour a night, so he had 23 in which to get stuff done. That was about a 7-hour advantage over the rest of us, and believe me, he put it to good use.
>
> He always wanted to play . . . with his family, with his friends, damn near anybody, and like when we were in Hawaii, he wanted you to play too. And like everything he did, it had to be on a grand scale. Lots of food, lots of laughs, lots of drinks. Like he used to tell me, "John, the problem with drinking is it makes you think you're invisible."

He really had a presence on a lot of personal levels with me. One time, I was in Raleigh covering a game, and I was moping around about some problem in my life, something with my job, or a woman, something like that. And he said, "Are you kidding me? You have the best #@!$$@#% life! What are you upset about? It's a great job, you're good at it, you love doing it. What's to be upset about? John, always remember, don't mess with happy."

Don't mess with happy. That about summed it up for Jim. His family heard it all the time, his friends heard it all the time, I heard it all the time. If things are good, stop analyzing and start living! Richie Petriccione once got the same advice:

> I remember I was trying very hard to get a head coaching job, as I was then the assistant at Florida State. I just couldn't seem to get one, and finally was close to being offered the Monmouth College job in New Jersey. I really went after it hard, and it came right down to the end, and I didn't get it. Next day, I get a call from V and he says, "Don't worry about it. Why would you want to coach at a school that means 'my mouth' in French?" He told me better things would come my way, and sure enough, not too much later, I got the athletic director's job at Iona. He made me laugh and feel better at a time I was really disappointed.
>
> You could always count on him to help you, but not always in the way you planned. I know once when he was at State, he was asked by a friend in the silk importing business if he would play golf with a guy from whom he imported ties, who was actually some sort of royalty in Italy. He was a count or something, but he knew basketball, and wanted to play with Jim. The guy asks Jim, who agrees, and they all head to the course: Jim, his friend, the count, and the count's friend.
>
> The first hole, the guy is a bit nervous, keeps waggling the club, and then hits it in the woods. He takes another ball, and just dribbles it about 50 feet in front of the tee. It's like this for the first two holes, and on the third hole, the count does it again. Waggle, waggle, swing, dribble, and V can't take it anymore. He says, "Boy, you sure do $#@%%$ suck! We're not going to have a whole day of this shit are we?" And the count

starts laughing his head off! Jim kept him in stitches the whole day, and he later said it was one of the greatest days of his life. Jim just had that effect on people.

Jim's ability to spin a great yarn also brought him closer to many people. John Feinstein:

> He was a great storyteller, as we all know. He used to tell about the time he was home, in bed, about 5:15 in the morning, and he was up, of course, hadn't been to sleep yet. He suddenly remembers that he hasn't yet done his radio show. He used to have a daily 10-minute radio show that he would do by dialing in to the station via an ISDN line in his office at State, and they would tape for airing the next morning. Well, he forgot this day, so he doesn't bother to change, he just gets in his car and heads back to his office. It's now about half past five, there is very little traffic, and he runs a red light. Sure enough, a cop pulls him over. "Where you going, Coach?" he asks.
>
> Jim says, "I have to do my radio show."
>
> "At 5:30 in the morning? C'mon, Coach. Really, where you coming back from?"
>
> Jimmy says, "I'm telling you, I'm going to my office to do my radio show."
>
> The cop interrupts him. "Have you been drinking?"
>
> Jimmy, who's angry enough that he had to go back at 5:30 in the morning to begin with, jumps out of the car, rips his coat open, and says, "Look! I have my pajamas on! Do you think I was out bar hopping in my pj's?" The policeman finally let him go, but not without getting a pretty good story to tell the boys back at the station house.

This was an incredibly exciting time in Jim's life, and he often shared his experiences with his family and friends. He took me with him the first time he did the David Letterman show, knowing what a huge fan I was, and we had a great time meeting Paul Schaffer and musical guests Chrissie Hynde and the Pretenders. Another time his daughters got mad at him and wouldn't speak to him for two days because he didn't give them a chance to meet Huey Lewis, who had stopped by for a visit after he finished rehearsing for a concert at N.C. State.

Jim was always amazed that other celebrities wanted to meet *him*. He called me one time after flying back from Los Angeles, and spending most of the flight talking with Jack Nicholson. He was dumbfounded because Nicholson had approached him, and while he had a million questions he wanted to ask about the movies, all Nicholson wanted to talk about was basketball. He never took any of that for granted, and his excitement was always contagious. In fact, he wanted *you* in on the fun.

He called me after his second appearance on *The Tonight Show* with Johnny Carson. Ever wonder what is said during those breaks where you see the host lean over to the guest? On this particular night, Jim leaned over and said, "I just wanted to thank you for having me back on again," and Johnny said, "Hey, we wouldn't do it if you weren't any #$@#!!%$ good."

Once when he was negotiating a new shoe contract, he kept calling me to give me periodic updates. The meetings were cordial but some of the finer points were rather complicated, and whenever the lawyers for both sides started with the boilerplate legal jargon Jim would dash out of the room and give me a call. "Wow, this is great, they just offered this and that," he said. "Oops, gotta go, they're calling me back." He called me back an hour later. "It's really getting close now," he said. "I think I really helped the process this last time. I told them about the time I went five-for-five against New Hyde Park at Seaford High School, including a three-run triple! I was standing on my chair telling them! They loved it! Oops, gotta go again." And he was off. He called back again. "Well, we got it done!" he said. "Although it got tough at the end. Just as we were about to sign the deal I said, 'I just remembered, I would really like one more thing.' They all rolled their eyes and said, 'Now what?' I said, 'I want you to send shoes to my brother's team. He's a Division II coach in Pennsylvania and they could really use the help.' They all breathed a huge sigh of relief. 'Is that all?' they said. 'No problem.'" And that year my Kutztown State College team had shoes, sweats, bags, the whole treatment, thanks to Jim and, I guess, going five-for-five against New Hyde Park, although I was never clear how that factored into the negotiations.

Clay Moser was impressed by how little Jim was changed by his new-found fame:

> I was amazed that Jim seemed completely undaunted by his celebrity. I mean, we would get polls back, and read articles, and his Q-rating would be off the charts. I remember sending

an article to recruits that showed the top 10 most recognizable sports figures by the magazine's poll. It was Jack Nicklaus, Magic Johnson, and V would be in the top 10! I'd be amazed, but V really didn't seem fazed by it, except for the fact that he thought it might help him get better recruits. That part of it *was* important to him.

In his time spent with V, Bob Costas also was witness to Jimmy's "lust for life":

> He had a passion for life that was just so appealing. I remember one time we had a running argument about what the proper punch line was for a certain joke, which we carried on for about three years. He would dissect it like he was dissecting a play. But he had as much passion for that as everything else in his life. And the passion was genuine.

Jim was an English major in college and a self-described lover of the language and of words themselves. *Newsday* columnist Steve Jacobson recalls that Jim used to demonstrate the magic and versatility of the English language with the simple sentence "I poked him in the eye yesterday." If you insert the word "only" before and after each word in the sentence, it provides eight new sentences, each with a completely different meaning. Try it. (Only I poked him in the eye yesterday. I only poked him in the eye yesterday. I poked only him in the eye yesterday. And so on.) One simple word conveys eight different ideas. I never forgot that, and the fact that an eloquent writer like Jacobson never did either speaks to the passion that Costas noted; Jim's spirit seemed to transcend professions, subject matter, and just about everything else. It was why it was so much fun to be around Jimmy, especially during those heady times.

It was a glorious run filled with success, laughs, experiences, and, for the ultimate "fun monkey," more fun than you could imagine. Still, Jim had trouble following his own advice. He "messed with happy," and things slowly started to turn, finally building to a crescendo of negative feelings and ill will. The end of the decade signaled the end of a magical run at N.C. State.

10

TOUGH TIMES

MOST PEOPLE KNOW THAT JIM WAS FIRED FROM HIS JOB AT N.C. STATE, and vaguely remember that there were some allegations of corruption, an investigation, and something to do with a book. I'd like to set the record straight and describe what really happened as best I can. Let me make it very clear from the beginning that the book, *Personal Fouls* by Peter Golenbock, did not get Jim fired, nor did the NCAA investigation.

The book was a bestseller. It made sensational accusations, painting the N.C. State program as one plagued with academic and financial fraud and corruption. It also hinted that the program was rampant with NCAA violations. Whatever merit the allegations may or may not have had, the book itself was riddled with careless inaccuracies and misstatements of fact: games played on wrong dates or in the wrong city, misspelled names, and other factual errors. Worse, many of the people quoted in the book as sources didn't actually meet the author until *after* the book was published.

How did the book come about? There were three main reasons. First, a manager named John Simonds became dissatisfied with his experience at State. He claimed he was promised a playing spot on the team, felt misled, and attempted to harm the program and specifically Jim, who was the target of his wrath. According to Jim, no such promises were ever made, and most of Simonds' dealings would have been with Ed McClain, the assistant coach who supervised team managers. Second, there were some disgruntled current and former players (as there are in every program): guys who didn't think they were getting enough playing time, or had other complaints. It is true that after winning the NCAA title, Jim and his staff, perhaps a bit overenthusiastically, went about getting absolutely the best players they could. They had an embarrassment of riches in talent, but not a great fit in terms of team chemistry. They also had some players who were, shall we say, "high maintenance," and Jim wasn't around as much as he should have been to watch over them. Problems were allowed to fester, and they found their way to Simonds, who was more than willing to exploit them to get back at a coach he felt had done him wrong. The third reason, however, is perhaps the most important. There are lots of unhappy managers and players in programs all over the country. Why did Golenbock focus on N.C. State? The answer is because Jim was such an easy target.

Even then it wasn't easy to get the book published. More than one writer turned Simonds down when approached, and after Golenbock had agreed, at least one well-known publisher backed out after agreeing to publish it because they were concerned about its accuracy.

At that time, college basketball was undergoing a transformation and becoming a big business, and as such had some very real and legitimate issues that needed to be addressed. By focusing his book on one of the most visible and flamboyant coaches in the sport—one who was thought by many to typify the "big business" aspect of the game—Golenbock was guaranteed great interest in it. There was a growing suspicion that, with all the money pouring into college basketball and all the side deals and business interests the big-time coaches had, there had to be *something* underhanded going on at N.C. State, and probably at other high-profile programs as well.

Events subsequent to the book's publication prove that it wasn't the cause of Jim's demise. As athletic director, Jim responded to the book's claims by immediately ordering a full NCAA investigation of his own program; he knew that the most serious accusations—misuse of $1 million in athletic department funds, grade changing, and drug tampering—were all simply untrue. In addition to the NCAA, the program was also investigated by the N.C. State Faculty Senate, the State Bureau of Investigation, and the "Poole Commission," a special committee appointed by the chancellor. After all these investigations, which made N.C. State's arguably the most scrutinized basketball program in history over a two-year period, the only significant violations found were that some players sold complimentary game tickets and their basketball shoes. That's it.

In fact, when the NCAA issued its final report, they indicated that no member of the staff had been found in violation. In the past, the NCAA had sanctioned individual coaches they felt were responsible for misdeeds. As there was no N.C. State staff member involved, there was no sanction made by the NCAA committee. Moreover, when Chuck Smrt of the NCAA investigative staff announced the results, he also indicated that State had gained "no clear and direct competitive advantage" by any of the infractions, which meant that the infractions were "minor" by NCAA standards. The NCAA did think the University needed to enhance its "institutional control," and therefore placed the program on probation, which curtailed postseason play for a year.

This move was significant because it showed that the University needed to do a more thorough job of monitoring aspects of its department; Jim in fact always said that the recommendations that came from the investigation were good and helpful. He regretted that it took an NCAA investigation for these problems to receive attention, but fully supported the important suggestions that came about as a result. The NCAA investigation was fair, and Jim found them to be professional, thorough, and interested in getting to the truth, not in creating a vendetta.

This was not so with some of the other groups examining the basketball program. In fact, many of these well-meaning people didn't have the background necessary to ask questions about intercollegiate athletics. Jim recalled one meeting with a member of the Poole Commission who asked him why the players would sell their shoes. Jim said for the money, of course, since many of them came from less than affluent backgrounds. The man then said, "You mean you don't pay the players?" Jim thought he was kidding, but he wasn't. Here was a member of the commission charged with investigating abuses in the basketball program who seriously thought that the players got paid. That was alarming, to say the least. Lots of people had their fingers in the pie, some with their own agendas to be sure, but many of even the best-intentioned investigators were clearly not versed in the subject they were being asked to explore.

Nevertheless, after more than a year of almost constant investigation, only two minor violations were found—the shoes and the tickets. It's safe to say that the NCAA investigation did not lead to Jim's firing.

What about the book? More than seven months into the various investigations, N.C. State Vice Chancellor Albert Lanier called *Personal Fouls* "a work of fiction." Yet two weeks later, he claimed that the University had changed its official position. What happened in those two weeks to make the school change its mind?

In July of 1989, Dr. Hugh Fuller, the head of State's academic tutoring program, charged that "Academic abuses and manipulation of rules to keep athletes eligible were . . . routine." By his own admission, the earlier publication of the book is what prompted Dr. Fuller to speak up at that particular time. Jim had worked with Dr. Fuller on several committees at State, and they had disagreed on how to motivate "at risk" students. Fuller had always been a quiet man, but Jim didn't fully appreciate how deep-seated his feelings were.

Fuller charged that athletes routinely abused the system to stay eligible. As evidence, he cited two players who had withdrawn from school for a semester for purported medical or psychological reasons, thus having that semester's grades wiped out. He also claimed that players shied away from more difficult professors and that coaches pressured professors into giving players certain grades.

Let's look at each of the three charges separately. First of all, even if two athletes did withdraw for a semester to avoid bad grades, two incidents in 10 years hardly constitutes a "routine" abuse, and one or both may well have been for legitimate reasons. The charge that athletes avoided the more difficult courses and professors? Wow, what a revelation! What are you going to tell us next, that it's hard for a school to fire an incompetent, tenured professor? Thanks, but we already knew that. The third charge needs to be looked at more closely because it's a sensitive area in which subjective judgments and interpretations often come into play. Jim told me that in 10 years at State he never called a professor because he specifically wanted to avoid the appearance of any "pressuring" for grades. However, his assistants would call or write professors to try to monitor the players' progress. Some faculty welcomed the interest and appreciated the support, but others were resentful of any attempt at all by someone from the athletic department to "invade" their realm.

As a relevant aside, I can tell you from my own experience at six different colleges of varying sizes and scholarship levels that at each and every one there were some professors who appreciated my efforts to communicate with them about student-athletes and some who definitely did not. I would send a memo to the various professors as an attempt to monitor our athletes' progress, and the responses ran the gamut. To some, it was just what they wanted—a coach who was demonstrably interested in his players' academic endeavors—while others wrote back with a warning never to contact them again, and a not so thinly veiled hint that they thought you were trying to influence grades. Same notes, same schools, same faculties, but extraordinarily different responses. The point is that *every* school has some faculty who resent athletics, and particularly the coaches. Often those coaches are more highly paid than the profs and are nationally celebrated and lionized by the media. Fuller, for his part, chose to highlight those professors who resented the coaches while ignoring the not insignificant number who appreciated and welcomed that contact.

Finally, Fuller took exception to student-athletes who asked for incompletes in courses they were having difficulty with. But this too is a common practice for athletes and nonathletes alike. Common sense dictates that a student isn't just going to passively accept an F if he or she can make up the work later or do additional assignments to raise the grade. This hardly seems like an earth-shattering revelation.

What made these charges significant was that Dr. Fuller was a respected member of the N.C. State academic community. There were people in various factions who felt Jim *was* getting a little too big for his britches, a little too powerful, a little too visible. They were looking for something they could use to bring him down a peg or two, and many of them were looking for vindication of their belief that there had to be *something* going on. The NCAA and the other investigations hadn't found anything of substance, and much of *Personal Fouls* had been discredited. Here was their chance! Fuller was one of N.C. State's own, and he had impeccable academic credentials, so Jim's opponents could rally behind him and his charges.

Even worse from Jim's point of view was that Fuller's accusations damned many others who were less in the spotlight. The implication that he was a "lone wolf" fighting for academic integrity was a slap in the face to the various deans, admissions officers, and other administrators who did not share Jim's high profile, but who could easily have felt as besmirched by Fuller's remarks.

The final assault came from the *Raleigh News and Observer*. I don't claim to be a neutral observer, since Jim after all was my brother, but it seemed to me and many others that the paper had an agenda and their coverage of events was less than fair. In fact, after Jim was fired, the soon-to-retire editor of the paper, Claude Sitton, was overheard to say that he wanted "one more scalp" before he left, and that scalp was going to be Jim's. Later, a former reporter for the paper approached me and said, "Even though you don't know who I am, I was working at the *News and Observer* at the time they were after your brother. I have felt ashamed all these years since that the newspaper that I worked at conducted itself that way."

There were so many aspects of this whole unfortunate period in Jim's career that one could easily write a study or a book about. What does it say about the relationship between athletics and academics? Between coaches and faculty? About the role the media plays in the hiring and firing of public figures? The chancellor, Dr. Bruce Poulton, a great friend and supporter of Jim's, lost his job over the episode, and in hindsight, that may have been one of the greatest injustices of all. It also reinforces the fact that academics was ultimately the key issue. Many basketball players with academic credentials far below the average N.C. State student had been admitted, and as a result there's no question that the graduation rate for the program was very low. It had been for some time, and in point of fact, compared to the overall rate for the general student population, it wasn't all that bad. For example, for all black males who enrolled at State in 1986, only 3.7 percent (eight students, to be exact) ended up graduating. The graduation rate was clearly part of a broader institutional problem that needed to be addressed, but when Jim called attention to that statistic, the faculty senate quickly issued a statement letting him and everyone else know that the spotlight would be shining only on the basketball program's graduation rate. From that point on, the only numbers that were discussed were those of the student-athletes, most frequently those of the basketball players. When the newspaper pointedly used only those statistics to try to "fan the flames," they got the desired result.

We won't revisit the numbers. Just keep in mind this quotation from Vin Scully: "People use statistics the way a drunk uses a lamppost: for support, not illumination." Jim did it too; he had numbers that strongly supported his argument that this was a campus problem, not just a problem in the athletic department. But he didn't have the ability to splash the numbers he wanted to focus on across four columns in 72-point type, as the *News and Observer* could.

Perhaps the best insights into the causes of Jim's problems come from those who knew him well. For instance, said Mike Krzyzewski:

> First, let's talk about what this was not. It was not about arrogance, and it really wasn't about money. I think Jim was very confident he could do a lot of things, but was he arrogant? No.
>
> As for the money, well, it was a factor, because you have to remember when we both started in the ACC. It isn't like it is now. My first contract with Duke was for $40,000 a year. Jim

was in much the same boat, so if someone said hey, I'll give you some money for a speech, or for a commercial, it was important for your family to be able to take those opportunities. I know Jim's background was a lot like mine: not poor, but far from rich. The opportunity to make a better life for your family comes along, no one can fault you for taking it. I mean, it wasn't like the University was saying, "Look, we don't want you doing all of those things, here's a $250,000 contract." No one said that.

That is how the money factors in, but so much of the stuff he was doing was not about money. That's why I say his problems weren't money driven. I think after he won the title, in all honesty, he got a little bored. He was looking for challenges, and he believed he could do so many different things—which he could—that he got involved with many of them, maybe too many of them. He was like an army fighting a war on too many fronts. Any of them individually he could win, but not all at once.

Jim did get involved in too many other things, but coaching was always his first love. He had many offers to do things outside basketball, and some were very intriguing. "But," he said, "you know why I don't leave? Because I've tried them all—TV, speeches, radio, business, books—but none of them, not one, gives me the same feeling as being on the sideline, coaching a basketball game. Nothing can take the place of that."

Frankly, that focused passion also caused a problem for Jim. The many other parts of coaching, which at the very least must be regarded as necessary evils, had little appeal for him. The administrative work bored him and, like most rational human beings, he didn't like recruiting. Film work is by its very nature tedious, and he certainly was not a lover of practice. However, as Coach K says, it would be unfair to say that Jim did a poor job in some of those areas just because he had little enthusiasm for them:

Jim had a reputation for being passionate about everything in his life, of which basketball was just a part. Because of that he was perceived, since he loved the games so much, as just being a great "game coach." And he was a good game coach, but he was a solid strategist, good with the *X*s and *O*s, a quick study when it came to analyzing opponents. The point was that he was good at many different parts of coaching, and he wanted to prove he was good at something else. What happens is you don't pay enough attention to dotting *I*s and crossing *T*s and eventually you have slippage. That is what happened to Jim.

Take Chris Washburn. He was a kid that everyone in hindsight says they never should have recruited. I strongly disagree with that. He was a great player, hundreds of other universities wanted him and would have taken him. The problem was, Jim was not around enough and a guy like Chris, with his limited academic background, needed more attention. Jim probably delegated that attention to someone, but *he* needed to be there, to be more hands-on, to take greater control of that situation.

What made it worse was that Jim was very high profile. This was one of the most sought after recruits in the country. Everyone was watching both of their every moves, and frankly, especially with Jim, there were people *looking* for something wrong. He wasn't from North Carolina. He didn't say, "y'all." He was "out there," maybe a bit too much: having a cigar, drinking some wine. Some people resented his celebrity. He needed to be aware of that, especially then. That's almost 20 years ago now, and this area was a lot more conservative.

What made it worse I think for Jim is that, while he could understand some of the criticism and say, "OK, I made some mistakes," he was pissed off that the implication was that he had to cheat to win. That would infuriate me, and I know it angered him too.

John Feinstein was also able to observe Jim's actions during this difficult time:

What makes it tough is that there were all these things being said, and people wanted Jim to stand up and say, "I take full responsibility. It's my fault." Jim wouldn't do that because he didn't believe all they were saying was true to begin with, and he certainly wasn't going to take the blame for every accusation. It's like when someone writes a critical review of one of my books. Say he makes 10 criticisms. Well, when I read the review, in my heart of hearts I might say, "You know, two of those things are probably true. The other eight are ridiculous but those two are valid." But when someone asks if so-and-so is right in the criticism of your book, it's hard to say yes because on 8 of the 10 points he was dead wrong. I think that's how it was with Jim.

The two things that bothered Jim the most were the accusations that he needed to cheat to win and that he really was not interested in the academic performance of his players. Here are two stories that illustrate why these were part of the "eight things ridiculously wrong," to paraphrase Feinstein. My mother was staying with Jim and his family once when a very prominent recruit came to the house for a visit. Jim had a huge walk-in closet where he stored the shoes, shirts, bags, and other promotional items provided to him and his team through his contract with Nike. The recruit and his parents were in the family room looking at the photos, awards, and other mementos around the room when one of them wandered into the "Nike closet," and came out passing around goodies for the whole family. They were having a good time and thought it was innocent enough, but when Jim saw what they had, he told them that unfortunately, if they wanted to keep the things, they'd have to pay for them, as it was a violation of NCAA regulations to give anything away. The mood changed quickly. They put almost everything back, paid for a couple of small things, like socks, by writing a check, and clearly were displeased by the turn of events. This was a very, very good player. No one was there to see any of this except my mother, who witnessed the whole thing. If ever you were going to "cheat" to gain an advantage with very little chance of anyone finding out about it, this would have been the time to do it. The recruit, by the way, wound up going to a different school.

The next instance took place shortly after Jim became athletic director at N.C. State, a position he accepted in addition to his basketball duties with no additional raise in pay. He was giving me a tour of the facilities and wanted to check on the football team in the weight room and introduce me to Dick Sheridan, the football coach. Jim seemed enthused about all the sports—men's, women's, revenue, nonrevenue—but what got him more revved up than anything else on my visit was showing me the new academic support center they were building at the time. He told me about the program and what a huge help it was going to be for all the student-athletes, what the building was going to be like, etc. Now I think I know my brother pretty well; we did, after all, share a bedroom for six years. And I can tell you that he was truly excited about this program even though it was just me there. There was no media, no one to impress; I was a small college coach at the time, not at ESPN. There was no reason to snow me. It was just me and him, and it was real.

People may justifiably find fault with the way some things were administered at N.C. State, but they are grossly unfair and presumptuous when they ascribe motives to Jim that simply were not true. He may have created some of his own problems—many of them, perhaps, by getting involved in too many "extracurricular" activities—but the accusations of cheating and lack of interest in academics are simply false. Said State's women's basketball coach Kay Yow:

> Doing too many things caused problems for Jim in ways you would not think of. For example, he was always being asked to make appearances, to say a few words, to shake some hands. People would call and say, "It's only for 10 minutes," but not realize that he might have literally 40 of those requests at any one time. It's never "just 10 minutes" and when you combine a number of those, it can be basically the whole day. Still, Jim hated to say no, so he'd try to cram in as many as he could.
>
> He might have a half hour free, right after practice, so he'd jump in the car, head over to the function, say a few words, and then go back to the office. That sounds like an admirable thing to do, but Jim would have shown up in his sweats, and people would interpret that as disrespect. It was their big night, and while they were all dressed up, here's their guest of honor in a sweat suit. Instead of realizing that might be the only way he could do it—and they weren't paying him to be there—they were upset that he showed up in a sweat suit. He probably would have been better served just to say no but, honestly, he just hated to say no to anything.

Jim's success and personality may also have turned some people against him. Said Mike Krzyzewski:

> I thought Jim was a victim of his own incredible profile—his demeanor, his publicity.

But that is who he was. If he could have just been a little understated, just a little bit, I don't think any of this would have happened. I mean the University should have stuck with him; they didn't do *anything*. That's what I was always amazed at, how quickly they bailed out on him, and for nothing! I think it showed just how envious people were over who he was; he was perceived as flashy, and he probably could have handled everything at a lower level, toned it all down just a bit, and still have been himself. I don't know if he had no one telling him to do that, or if he did and he just ignored their advice.

I learned from his experience. The way his success in a way jumped up and bit him made me aware it could happen to any of us. If you are successful and high profile, there will always be someone out there looking to take you down and, even though our situations were different, I became much more sensitive to that after seeing what Jim went through.

Jim probably didn't take care of some relationships that could have helped him; he didn't spend enough time with people who were important to what he was doing there. But still, the whole episode was completely out of whack. It should never have reached the proportions it did. I talked to him while it was going on, and told him I couldn't believe that this was going to cost him his job. He wasn't cheating. It all seemed so small, but image was important, especially around here. Former North Carolina coach Dean Smith had such a different style . . .

I think Jim was just too brash, especially then for some people, and they were determined to make a huge issue out of some relatively small things.

Kay Yow also thought that misconceptions about Jim's personality were at the heart of some of his problems:

I think people made assumptions about Jim that hurt him. For example, he was always so "on," with such a wellspring of energy about him, that people thought there couldn't be much depth there. His ability to be clever could be misconstrued. To some, clever has a bad connotation. He was loud, he had plans; people used to say he was a schemer. The point is, they really didn't know him, but based their opinion on a glimpse of Jim here, a sound bite there. And he certainly was visible, there's no doubt about that.

I think he really liked to give people a chance and thought he could really make a difference in some kids' lives. You know, I'm not really sure we *can* change people. But Jim wanted to try, and he had confidence he could help, and we would see a change in that young man, we could move him in a different direction. The problem was that it became a lot of kids who you could call "high maintenance" and he wasn't always able to provide that maintenance.

Friends in the media, such as John Feinstein, observed some of the same problems. Here Feinstein also talks about how Jim's problems put his media friends in a difficult position:

It was simply not the best way to choose to do it. If he was going to recruit high-maintenance people, he needed to do less things away from basketball. If he wanted the kind of kid you don't have to sit on, he had to spend more time recruiting that kind of kid. And he needed to be hands-on with his support people. Without that, there are a lot of little things that slip through the cracks.

What made it worse is I really think when it came to the media, Jim was a bit naïve. He was quotable, funny, a hell of a coach, and had won the national championship. All of a sudden when things escalated and there were some legitimate concerns about who was minding the store, Jim took offense when people wanted him to stand up and say, "This is my fault." I don't think he was capable of it initially, and as it grew, it became impossible to separate the things he'd be willing to take responsibility for from those he thought were absurd.

By the end, I wrote about one of his last meetings with the press where he just rambled on for over an hour, and I said he sounded "Nixonesque." He didn't talk to me for a long time after that column. From his point of view, he felt there were already people out there making wild accusations about who he was who didn't even know him, maybe had never even met

him. That is not unusual—probably 95 percent of the time
people write or comment about a public figure, they don't
know them. But Jim felt that his "friends" in the media, at least
the guys who knew who he was, should have given him more.

Maybe he was right, but it was tough. He needed to take
some responsibility, and he wasn't doing it.

In response to that charge, I can only say (as Jim said after it was all over)
that there is a distinction between "responsibility" and "culpability." As the
guy in charge, Jim said all along he was culpable, but he was quick to point
out that he didn't feel responsible. In hindsight, I think he would agree with
Mike and Kay that he *was* responsible for some of it, certainly for doing too
many things at once. I once heard him tell our mother, who was lambast-
ing the press for being too critical of her son, "Ma, I did this. It was my fault
too." So he certainly came to appreciate his own role in all his problems.

But if we were to summarize what happened at State, in reality, it was
this: a program where the only NCAA violations were selling tickets and
shoes suddenly had what had been private academic records made public.
As a result, people became acutely aware of the fact that basketball players were less than stellar students, and had been for a long time. A high-
profile coach became the target of resentment by a part of the community, the newspaper made it their No. 1 cause célèbre, and Jim felt he was
being made the scapegoat for a University-wide problem regarding the
academic achievement of student-athletes. He was also being asked to
admit to motives he knew he didn't have. His friends in the media
"turned" on him as well, interpreting his refusal to accept the scapegoat
role as a denial of any responsibility whatsoever. Finally, he was fired with
a cloud of suspicion hanging over his head.

One person who thought he got to know Jim pretty well throughout
the ordeal was Dave Dideon, the NCAA investigator. One would think
this would be an adversarial relationship at best, and it was initially
uncomfortable. But as they got to know each other, some good things
developed. Jim began to put a human face on the organization, to see that
the NCAA was not "Big Brother" and that they suffered from the same
problem as he did: people ascribed motives to them without really knowing very much about them. At the same time, Dideon got to know Jim
Valvano the man, not the public figure. When the investigation was over,
Dideon wrote Jim a letter. In it, he said:

Before I met you, I thought I might encounter some smart-ass egomaniac who would try to bullshit me. Those impressions vanished after I met you and spent some time around you. If I had a son, I would be proud to have him play for you.

From adversity often comes a blessing, as that letter was for Jim at a very trying time.

Jim also believed that, like everything else in life, the scandal surrounding him at N.C. State could provide a rich source of amusement. We'll end this chapter with several examples. The plight of Jim Valvano became such a national story and the allegations, usually unsubstantiated, were so endless that it bordered on the absurd. At least that's how some saw it. . . . In *NCSU Today*, an N.C. State April Fool's day spoof of *USA Today*, the following item appeared:

WEATHER: According to sources at Raleigh's *News and Observer*, recent snow and rain in the Rockies and the Northeast; thunderstorms in the Midwest and South Central; all to be blamed on Jim Valvano.

WALL STREET: Dow drops 15.99 . . . *News and Observer* claims Valvano to blame.

OZONE HOLE: Sources at Raleigh's *News and Observer* cite hearsay linking Valvano to 1000-mile hole.

USA'S HOMELESS: America's homeless top 28 million . . . point fingers at Coach V . . . resignation only solution.

CHALLENGER DISASTER: NASA, unaware of *News and Observer*'s Valvano bashing, deny N.C. State coach designed faulty O-ring.

Local media were not the only ones to poke fun at Jim's dilemma. On *Saturday Night Live*'s "Weekend Update," Dennis Miller reported: "SNL news has learned that the stock market crash of '87, the Greenhouse Effect, and the Vietnam War were all caused by . . . Jim Valvano." And when actor Robin Williams was asked about not winning the Oscar for the film *Dead Poets Society* on a national radio program, he said, "I blame it on Jim Valvano."

Still, all humor aside, these were dark days for Jim. He was terminated as basketball coach at N.C. State on April 7, 1990.

11

IN THE BROADCAST BOOTH

WHEN JIM WAS FIRED AT N.C. STATE, PEOPLE WERE ALMOST universally critical of him and his program. He was regarded as selfish, ambitious, unconcerned with academics, and in charge of a program rampant with NCAA violations, a program that typified all that was wrong with college athletics. I hope it's clear from the preceding chapter that much of this was either greatly exaggerated or simply not true. While Jim was far from a choirboy, he certainly wasn't the greedy, self-serving egomaniac his vitriolic critics made him out to be. During those difficult days, he became a convenient whipping boy for all that was perceived to be wrong with college sports.

And make no mistake about it, those were very difficult days. Not only would no other college consider hiring him, even the media outlets were taking a hands-off approach. His public speaking opportunities had dried up almost completely. In short, almost all the things that Jim did in his professional life—coaching, speaking, and broadcasting—were closed to him. All gone.

Jim had all his usual energy and nowhere to channel it. Later, he would look back on these days, reflecting on *The Tonight Show* with Johnny Carson that he had become a couch potato. He started ordering all sorts of things from TV infomercials: the sandwich maker, the Veg-O-Matic and other kitchen gizmos, and finally the "Flowbee," a gadget that connects to a vacuum so you can give yourself a haircut at home. He knew it was time to try to get his life back together when, while using the Flowbee, he overheard one of the girls say to Pam, "Mom, Dad is vacuuming his head. . . ." It was time to regroup.

Jim was an inveterate collector of quotations, and his favorite was from Albert Schweitzer:

> In everyone's life, at some time, the inner fire goes out. It is then burst into flame by an encounter with another human being. We should all be grateful for those people who rekindle our inner spirit.

Make no mistake: Jim's inner fire was out and he needed someone to rekindle it. That someone turned out to be Dennis Swanson, the head of ABC Sports. Jim's agent, Arthur Kamensky, had been in touch with Swanson about the possibility of hiring Jim, even though the other networks wouldn't touch him. Swanson called ABC Sports producer Geoff Mason and asked him what he thought. Geoff had never met Jim, but he still had some concerns:

> Dennis called me and said he wanted to bounce something off me, which he often did. He said, "We got a call from Art Kamensky. He wants us to meet Jim Valvano, and I think he's going to put in a formal request to ask for our consideration [about hiring Jim]." I said something like, "Holy shit Dennis . . . what do you think we should do?" Because this was when the whole Jimmy V story had hair all over it. I had been reading what people were saying about this guy. I knew we were going to take a hit if we hired him. Take a hit? Get murdered in the press would actually be more like it. "I just don't know . . ." I said.
>
> Dennis said, and I'll never forget this, "If we let this one go, we will never forgive ourselves."
>
> I said, "You know what? You're right. Let's go for it."
>
> Dennis had an uncanny ability to recognize potential; he is the one who discovered, for example, Oprah Winfrey. In fact, when Oprah wins an award, she often still thanks Dennis Swanson. So, much as I would like to take credit for "discovering" Jimmy V, the broadcaster, it was really Dennis and his belief in Jim's potential. I was there in the first discussions, but I really give credit to Swanson. I will say this, though; from the moment I started working with Jim, getting to know him, and

going on the road with him, there was never a doubt in my mind he was going to be very good. Not one doubt.

A guy who ultimately grew to respect Jim's broadcasting ability and became one of his closest friends was ESPN commentator John Saunders. He too had never worked with Jim before they were paired to do some games and studio work for ESPN. He recalls the first time they met:

Well, here we are on our first night working together. I don't know Jim at all, and he certainly doesn't know me. I have been reading all these things about him in every paper in America though, so I really don't know what to think about who he really is. We decide to go out after the show for a beer to visit, get to know each other better, and I'm hoping to find out what Jim is really like. We go to a little pub near ESPN, and the place is pretty empty. Jim and I are just starting to talk, and he's basically saying, "You know, they've written a lot of things about me . . . but you just make up your own mind." He's painting himself as just a regular guy, and that's what he seems to be, but in the back of my mind are all the sensational things that were written, so I'm trying to decide.

All of a sudden a woman who had been standing at the bar with a biker friend comes over to Jim. She says she knows who he is, and Jim is polite, and making small talk. Then she says—completely out of the blue—that she would like to take Jim into the back room and, shall we say, "entertain" him. This is certainly a bit unusual to say the least. Now Jim is getting a bit nervous. The biker guy is a big, nasty-looking fellow, and Jim is wondering if he knows his girlfriend is hitting on him. Jim stammers out a refusal of her offer, and encourages her to go back to her boyfriend at the bar, not wanting to rile the big fellow up.

The woman walks away, and I'm thinking that for an "average Joe," this guy I'm with sure has some unusual things happen to him. I hadn't seen *that* happen all that often in my time at ESPN, but little did I know things were just getting started. The woman comes back with her biker friend, and both Jim and I think, "Uh, oh. He heard what she said, and here comes trouble."

Instead, he comes over, and says, "She told me what she said to you, and I just wanted you to know, it's OK by me. I don't mind. You go ahead and have some fun." Now I'm really dumbfounded. Here is a guy offering this girl—his wife, girlfriend, whatever—to Jim! With his blessings! In a bar, one of the first times Jim has ever been to Bristol, Connecticut.

Again, Jim kind of stammers out a "thanks, but no thanks." I see him looking out of the corner of his eye at me as if to say, "Really, this kind of thing doesn't normally happen to me!" while the other two are obviously serious, and waiting for an answer.

Jim, ever polite, thanks the guy, but explains that his "blessing" really wasn't the issue here, and that he is not interested, thank you very much. The girl looks really disappointed, and asks if he would at least sign something for her. Jim says sure. And with that, she lifts up her shirt and asks him to sign her breast! At this point my jaw is around my knees, but Jim doesn't even hesitate. He takes a Sharpie, and signs, "Dick Vitale."

According to Geoff Mason, Jim was practically a broadcasting natural:

Jim's first assignment for ABC Sports was to cover the Harlem Globetrotters with Lynn Swann. We were at Disney World in Florida, and we were in our first production meeting. I was the executive producer, and I was going over the sequence of plays. I told Jim and Lynn, "Your guests will be Mickey Mouse, Minnie Mouse, and Miss Piggy."

Then we had one of those great TV moments. A Disney executive said, "Wait a minute. We aren't promising Miss Piggy. The mice, fine. We can get Mickey and Minnie. But Miss Piggy? I'm not sure about that."

"Hold it," I said. "I thought we were getting the pig. I thought it was all set." The Disney people said, "Tell you what . . . if we can't get Miss Piggy, we're sure we can get Pluto or Chip and Dale, and maybe Goofy too." But I was steadfast. We were promised Miss Piggy.

Jim just sat there, silently, unusual as that may seem, until I finally asked him, "Jim, what do you think?" Without missing a beat, he said, "I think we should hold out for the entire pig package." I cracked up, and remember thinking to myself, "This guy gets it. He is never going to take himself too seriously at all this, and that's good."

Jim's abilities quickly became obvious to John Saunders as well:

> What made him good was his ability to think on his feet and to come up with something quickly. Like the time we were doing the University of Cincinnati game. I was doing the play-by-play and Jim was doing the analysis. It was late in the game, and Bob Huggins, the Cincinnati coach, called timeout.
>
> Now Bob has become a good friend of the V Foundation, and does a lot of things to help. He is a good guy with a generous heart. Having said that, though, his vocabulary can be a bit, shall we say, colorful. Well, we decide to put their camera in their timeout huddle. I say something like, "Let's listen in on the Bearcats and see what Bob Huggins has to tell his team." For the entire minute or so of the timeout, Huggins is just attacking them, really letting them have it, talking a blue streak that would make a sailor wince. The whole timeout. And our camera and microphone have picked up the whole thing.
>
> The timeout ends, the huddle breaks, and it's back to Jim and me. There is an awkward silence . . . I mean, what can you say after an embarrassing tirade like that, heard by millions of viewers? Finally, Jim is the first to speak and he says, "You know John, there is such a thing as 'tough love.'" It was hilarious; it was perfect; and it saved what had been a very awkward moment.

According to Geoff Mason, Jim became one of the greats of sportscasting:

> Let me say this. Once Jim decided to just be himself on the air, he was great. He has one of those rare—and I do mean rare—personas where just by being yourself you're going to be successful. There are only two other guys besides Jim that I worked with that are like that: Howard Cosell and Bud

Collins. I think John Madden is like that too. These are people who were interesting people themselves, and once they were able to bring that to the air, they were great. I have worked with a lot of very, very good people, but that to me is what I call a "pantheon of excellence." Not many people go there, but I think Jimmy V did.

I mean, come on, we've all seen that tape of him kissing Dick Vitale during the pregame. Who else could do that? Think about it . . . live on national television, to just up and kiss your broadcast partner *on the air*? No one else could have done it then, and no one else could do it now. It's just who he was. He was funny and smart and he brought that to the air.

He did have to learn, though. At first, I don't think he appreciated the preparation that goes into doing a game. I know one of the first games, he was unfamiliar with some of the names. I told him that was part of his job—names, numbers, and pronunciations. I never asked how he did it, but from then on, he found a way to prepare. You only had to tell him once; he was a quick study. And curious! Perhaps the most curious individual I have ever met. Truly interested in just about anything, but it served him well in learning broadcasting.

I'll tell you something he did that no other "talent" has ever done with me. He said to me after a game once, "Look, Geoff, I know you're not supposed to allow people in the production trucks while a game is on, but maybe you can sneak me in there for a game, just so I can watch. If I can learn what it is these guys are doing, I will have a better understanding of what *I* should do." He wanted to understand the process, to know who these guys were that were talking in his headset, and what it was they were trying to do. Very smart. I think every on-air guy should do that once, so they understand the process.

In only two short years of broadcasting, Jim won a "Cable Ace" award for sportscasting excellence. He was also nominated for an Emmy, and came to be regarded as a bright and upcoming star in the world of broadcasting. People, often begrudgingly at first, began to respect his ability as a broadcaster, and only the hardest of hearts could have failed to be swayed by his obviously sincere passion for the game and the people in it.

Schools began to sound him out about the possibility of returning to coaching again. Wichita State made him a very generous offer, which he finally declined after much deliberation. Then he called me one day and said, "I think I might get offered the New Jersey Nets job. Rick Pitino said he wasn't interested and he recommended me." I asked him if he would take it, and he replied, "I don't know. We've already had a family crisis about it. Pam said she's not moving back to New Jersey, and the girls have told me in no uncertain terms they're not moving *anywhere*. But I'm still interested. I'll let you know." A few days later he called back and said, "If they offer it, I think I'm going to take it. I'll just get an apartment in New Jersey and we can keep our house in Carolina. The girls can finish school there, Pam won't have to move, and it'll all work out."

Half kiddingly, I said, "When do I start?" I had been coaching for about 14 years at that point and my Catholic University team was on its way to its first 20-win season, but still, you don't often jump from Division III basketball to the NBA, so I really didn't expect him to take me seriously. He said, "I'll hire you. There are a lot of entry-level jobs you could do. Then maybe if you work hard and learn, you could become an assistant . . . that could work."

I was dumbfounded and thrilled. I had only worked with my brother one other time, about three months earlier, in the summer of 1991. Jim took a group of all-stars on a short European tour for Nike that summer and asked me if I wanted to come along and be his assistant. As part of the promotional deal, Charles Barkley, Scottie Pippen, and David Robinson were also going to make the trip, though only Pippen and Barkley would play, and they only in one game in Germany. I had an unforgettable time, and even in that odd setting, and in only 10 days together, I was amazed by how much I learned.

We had only two practices before we left and then four games in Europe, but Jim was a quick study of the talent he had available and how to make the best use of it. He put a couple of simple sets and plays in, and with just those, we were able to get the ball into whoever's hands we wanted, where we wanted it. Simple and efficient. He put a couple of zones in, although as you might guess we played mostly man to man. It was the defense that frustrated him the most. He liked to play around defensively, trying different things, playing some combination defenses based on the talent he had. There clearly was no time for that on this trip. Still, all in all he put in a remarkable "system" given that he had had just one week of preparation.

Barkley was a source of endless amusement on the trip. Everybody loves Charles. Jim did, and I do too. He's a very funny guy and has a heart the size of a house, though he may not want you to know that. We were playing the German League champions, Bayern Leverkeusen, in our first game. They had a big, enthusiastic crowd, and the game was on TV. It was close, though we led most of the way. Barkley and Pippen had each played for about 10 minutes in the first half, and about the first 8 minutes or so of the second half. When they came out, our lead started to evaporate, and with 6 minutes to go we found ourselves down by five points. It was late August, the off season for the NBA guys, and Jim wasn't sure how many minutes they wanted to play, so he somewhat tentatively asked Barkley and Pippen if they wanted to go back in. Barkley jumped up and yelled, "Damn right we're going back in! Why the hell you think we're here?"

With that they went back in and took over the game. Pippen took off from about the foul line on a fast break for a dunk, and Barkley, who looks a lot closer to 6'4" than 6'6", started going to the low block and just posting up everyone in Germany. We won by about 8 or 10 points, and afterward there was a big press conference. They asked Barkley what he thought when Bayern had come back to take the lead. "I thought," said Sir Charles, "here's this guy [meaning Jim] losing the game with $25 million worth of talent sitting on the bench. I thought, 'What the hell is *he* thinking?'" Everyone, including Jim, laughed at that one.

Then a reporter asked about the upcoming Olympics, to be held in Barcelona the following year, when the United States would send pros, the first of its "Dream Teams." Jim answered diplomatically, saying that the international competition was getting much better, and while the NBA players should be heavy favorites, the Dream Team would be good for the game and its popularity around the world. Then they asked Barkley the same question. He said, "I can't wait, because we're gonna kick everybody's a** by about 30 points and then I won't have to answer that stupid question any more." Fortunately, everybody laughed again.

We were 2–2 on the trip, but should have been 3–1. My small contribution was to help us lose an overtime game to George Karl's Real Madrid team, a game we should have won. We were up by three with five seconds to go and they were inbounding from their own backcourt, so they had the length of the court to go. They called timeout. Jim wanted to foul immediately so that, worst case, they'd make two free throws and the game would be over. But I argued against that. I had coached in Europe for a season and knew that officials there called intentional fouls much more often. The penalty was two shots *and the team got the ball back*, so I was worried they'd call an intentional foul, make two free throws, and still have a chance to win the game in regulation. I said, "No, a foul with these officials is too risky. Let's just defend the line."

Jim reluctantly agreed, though I knew he really thought fouling was the better strategy. He told the guys to basically ignore anyone inside the three-point arc and just concentrate on defending outside the line. Buzzer. Huddle breaks, the other team inbounds. Guards start up the floor, five . . . four . . . three . . . the dribbler goes off a ball screen and we just switch it . . . so far so good. Then he dribbles inside the arc and drives down the lane! I think we've won! He has nowhere to pass it and he's inside the three-point line! Just then, one of our guards comes racing in the lane from the weak side. The Real Madrid player jumps in the air, turns, and throws the ball backward to the weak side, and just before the buzzer the three-point shot is released. Nothing but net. Tie. Overtime. I feel sick. Needless to say, we lose in overtime, and all night long all I hear is Jim saying over and over, "We should have fouled. We should have fouled."

There's another memory from that trip that I've especially treasured. When we got to Limoges, France, we stayed in a hotel that, while far from plush, had its own golf course. This was great! We had no clubs (we certainly hadn't anticipated playing golf on this short trip), but how can you turn down the chance to play golf in France? We headed out to the course—Jim, myself, and our trainer, Gary Bonnewell, who is an old college friend of mine. Gary and I spoke not a syllable of French, and Jim not much more, though he took a year of it in college. But he was our only hope, so he went to what passed for a pro shop to pay the greens fees and let the starter know we needed to rent clubs.

Now, in general, I would try to avoid stereotypes, but in this case I must perpetuate one. The French are uncompromising when it comes to forcing other people, especially Americans, to speak their language. It would seem to be relatively simple to communicate—after paying the man to play golf and showing him through various gestures and swinging motions that we had no clubs—that we needed clubs, and were even willing to pay extra to rent them. But no! We had to grovel and play charades until we could find *something* approximating the sound of each of the

actual words in French in order to satisfy the haughty Frenchman's sense
of superiority. Jim would try certain words, and if he got one right, or
something close to it, the guy would repeat it, or at least acknowledge it
with a grunt. If not, he wouldn't say or do anything! Nothing! This went
on for about 20 minutes, even though the guy obviously knew what we
wanted all along.

We finally got three sets of clubs, but we had no golf balls and the pro
shop didn't sell any. Fortunately, another guy who had been watching our
little game of charades came over and gave us exactly four balls. Four balls
for the three of us! Talk about pressure! There was a lot of laying up and
playing safe that day.

As I said earlier, big brother was always able to beat me at almost anything; but the one game where I was able to hold my own was golf. In fact,
I usually beat him more than he beat me. But on this day, with 50-year-
old clubs probably used by Francis Ouimet and four golf balls between us,
he and I were playing pretty even. We got to hole 17, a par-3, with me up
by a stroke, and Jim hits a safe tee shot just short of the green. I sliced one
beyond the green and behind a tree, and was only able to chip to the back
fringe about 60 feet from the cup. With my "Tom Morris" signature put-
ter, I'm probably looking at 3-putting for a 5, while Jim has chipped to
within 10 feet and can make par. Here we go again . . . he's announcing his
comeback while I'm left to go crying to Mommy.

Well, I hit that putt and it went up a hill, and down a hill, and rolled
and rolled, and then rolled some more. As it got closer to the hole, I started chasing it because it looked like it was going to get pretty close. By the
time it reached the hole, I was practically at a dead sprint, and when it
went in, I started dancing and yelling and rolling on the green. I felt like
I had just won the NCAA championship. It must have been a hilarious
sight because when I looked up, both Jim and Bonnewell were doubled
over laughing. I didn't care. All I cared about was that I beat Jim.

Perhaps no other story better captures my brother's impact on my
life than the one about that trip. I learned a lot about basketball, certainly.
I learned a lot about France and Germany too, since Jim, as usual, had a
million questions. I laughed so hard my sides hurt. I learned about
life. And playing a round of golf on a nondescript course with obsolete
clubs and only one golf ball, I had one of the most memorable afternoons
of my life. When I think of that trip, I remember how irreplaceable Jim
is in my life.

/ / /

We took that trip three months before the Nets job became a possibility. The day after that second phone call from Jim about the NBA job, my team had a Saturday afternoon game. At halftime my wife, Darlene, stopped me as I was headed to the locker room. She *never* did that. This was literally the only time she did that in my 20 years of coaching. She said, "Your brother called, and he is frantic. And furious. Call him right after the game." Fortunately our team was pretty good that year, and we were winning easily; I was in a daze for most of the second half and didn't help them much. What had happened to Jim? After the game and my postgame responsibilities, I went to my office and called him. "What happened?" was about all I was able to get out, and he went crazy.

"Did you tell anyone about the Nets thing?" he demanded. He had warned me not to say anything to anybody because they had not formally made the decision to replace Bill Fitch. Then, when it looked fairly certain, they didn't want to announce it because it was just a couple of days before Christmas; so everybody was supposed to keep it absolutely quiet.

Jim went on, "I got to ESPN today and there's a report that I'm going to get the job. I'm about to go on the air for a game here and ESPN says, 'We can't put you on the air without a comment from you about this report. We'll lose all our credibility.' The Nets ownership said if I said so much as a word to the press about it, the deal was off. I tried to call them to tell them it wasn't from me. Did you tell anyone?"

"No," I lied. He knew I had told Darlene, but she certainly hadn't said anything. What he didn't know is that in my excitement I had also told our trainer, Karl Bailey. Had he told someone?

"Well, the Nets are very angry and embarrassed and it looks like it isn't going to happen now," Jim said. And it didn't. But even Jim himself later said that it might have been for the best. He always wondered whether or not he'd have made a good NBA coach, despite the enjoyment he got from hanging around players in the league. Still, I was heartbroken; for me, it was the opportunity of a lifetime. I was equally fearful that it had been my slip with Bailey that let the cat out of the bag. But Jim found out later that it was actually an ESPN colleague who, overhearing one of his phone calls, in turn called a friend in the print media.

We all have "what-ifs" in our lives, and that lost opportunity is mine. I spent 10 days as Jim's assistant and honestly feel it was such an educational and inspiring experience that my team went on that year to the best season in the school's history. What might I have learned in a year or two of working with him at the NBA level!

Sadly, this incident was not to become much of a "what-if" in Jim's life. While on a trip to Spain to do a World League of American Football (now just NFL Europe) game for ABC, Jim was on a golf course in Barcelona. He was standing on the tee box admiring the view when he suddenly felt a pain like he had never felt before. He had been having back pain for a few months, and had actually gone to a doctor earlier, but no one, including him, thought it was anything serious. This pain was different though, and he was determined to get to a doctor as soon as he got back to the States.

First though, in Barcelona, he had to—just *had* to—put on a Velcro suit, leap off a mini trampoline, and stick to a wall also covered in Velcro. It was part of the telecast from Spain, but Jim would have done it anyway. As he said later, "How can you go to Barcelona with the chance to stick to a Velcro wall and not do it?"

It might have been the last moment of innocent fun he ever had. When he returned to the States and went to the doctor, the news was not good.

12

"I'm Gonna Die..."

CHICAGO BULLS FANS MAY REMEMBER THE YEARS 1991, 1992, AND 1993 for the first of the team's "three-peats." I'll remember them for quite a different reason, since they were among the most gut-wrenching and emotionally draining periods my family and I ever went through. Early in 1991 we found out that my mother had heart disease; we took her in for an angioplasty, a relatively safe procedure in which a balloon is inserted in an artery to increase the flow of blood. Unfortunately, a small nick was made in one of the arteries and she began bleeding internally. Before the doctors were able to determine the source of the internal bleeding and stop it, her blood pressure had dropped to something like 80/20, and she nearly died.

That, however, was just a harbinger of the crazy things to come. While Mom was recovering, we all went through the wackiness of the New Jersey Nets situation. Shortly thereafter, Mom started to feel bad again. A reexamination showed that the arteries had become blocked once more and she was going to need heart bypass surgery.

As we waited for the surgery date to be set, the college basketball season ended in the spring of 1992. My Catholic University team had gone 20–6, the best record in the school's history, and had received a lot of local publicity in the Washington area because of our style of play. We had broken six NCAA records for three-point shooting, so despite being a small college program we got a lot of attention. That's significant, because just a couple weeks after the end of the season, and a few days before my mother's operation, Catholic decided to fire me. It was stunning news, and in Washington, at least, it became a very hot topic. It was the lead story on the evening news for several nights and the topic of radio call-in shows. People at first paid attention because after a 20-win season, there just *had* to be some juicy scandal behind the decision. Plus it was Jimmy V's brother! What had *he* been doing?

As it turned out, very little. Nothing to be proud of, certainly, but a series of relatively minor (in most people's minds) transgressions, which had been blown well out of proportion. What it really was, in fact, was a classic personality conflict. I clearly had some folks at Catholic who disliked me. Because of the odd circumstances it became a hot topic of conversation for the better part of two weeks.

My mother's condition was so sensitive that we decided not to tell her about my problem, and even though she was in New York and the story was reported there, we were able to keep it from her. In addition to all this, my wife's father had Alzheimer's disease, which had progressed to a point where he had to be put in a nursing home, and that just about broke Darlene's heart. So there I was, in a highly publicized firing, unable to share my humiliating burden with a mother I had always relied on, and with a wife who was in no position to offer much support because of the emotional distress she was experiencing with her own father.

Not surprisingly, I turned to my brothers for support, and to Jim in particular. I really wanted to coach again and needed his guidance and expertise to figure out what to do. He was always able to help me keep things in perspective. We had a three-year-old son and had just used all our savings to buy a house. Now we had no money and I had no job. Add those factors to everything else that was going on, yeah, I'd say I needed some perspective. Jim kept repeating to me one of his favorites from Brother Driscoll at Iona: "Nobody died. Take it easy . . . we'll get through it."

The worst day for me came right after my mother had her surgery. She looked so frail, so weak, so horrible that I almost couldn't stand it any more. When they wheeled her into the recovery room, with all the other things that had been happening, I had all I could do to hold back the tears. Jim came over and said, "I know you can't stand to see her like this, but you have to remember something. This is how *all* the patients look after they've had this procedure. Relax, she's going to be fine. And stop worrying about your problems. They'll all work out too. When? I don't know, but they will, and you'll be fine." I felt like I was back in high school again after the junior prom, but he made me feel better.

Sure enough, very quickly my mother began to regain her strength, soon saying she felt better than she had in years. She said if she had known she was going to feel so much better, she would have had the surgery sooner. And at Catholic, two law professors on the faculty, Mike Cozzillio and Lou Barracato, decided to represent me pro bono in an appeal. In addition, *Washington Post* columnist Tony Kornheiser wrote an article assessing the basis for my firing; one of my favorite lines from it was, "People don't get fired for these things in 1992. Or 1892. Or 1492." Things were looking up. The general public perception of my situation had changed and I was beginning to feel more hopeful. My mother's health was improving and Jim's career was going great.

In May 1992, we were home in Maryland. My mother had been out of the hospital for a while, and my appeal at Catholic was progressing well. The phone rang and it was Jim. We had been speaking frequently, but as soon as he got on, I knew something was very wrong. He was having trouble talking, and then he was simply sobbing. I couldn't figure out what it was. My mother? The girls? Nick? What?

He said, "I just got back from the hospital. They told me I have cancer . . . and I'm gonna die." Just then one of his daughters must have come into the room and heard him. I heard her piercing scream, and Jim putting down the phone, rushing to comfort her. "I'm sorry . . . I'm sorry. . . ."

I can't remember anything else from that day.

/   /   /

After the initial feeling of despair, Jim's natural buoyancy took over and his mood improved quickly. He was going to fight in every way possible.

My cousin's husband had an apartment in Manhattan that he used for business purposes, and he gave Jim and his family the use of it when they came to town for Jim's treatments at Sloan Kettering Hospital. Jim left nothing to chance. He practically shaved his head so that his hair wouldn't fall out from chemotherapy. He was going to beat it to the punch. He got fit for a hairpiece so that if his hair *did* fall out, he could still go on TV and work.

We were all part of Jim's "team." He had cards printed up that read:

Victories

I, _____ am a member of Valvano's
Incredible Cancer Team of Really Important
Extraordinary Stars.

The rules, printed on the back, said:

EVERY DAY I WILL:
1. Say to myself, "Jimmy V, you will make it."
2. Say out loud, "Jimmy V, hang in there."
3. Ask God to help Jimmy V.
4. Do something to strengthen myself mentally,
physically, and spiritually.
WELCOME TO THE TEAM!

Jim began treatment and continued to work on TV as if nothing had changed, while my own emotional roller-coaster ride continued. In August I won a settlement from Catholic for $30,000, was reinstated as coach, and promptly resigned. I was able to get another coaching job at a fine school, St. Mary's College of Maryland, where my good friend Jay Gardiner was the athletic director. Like me, he was one of three boys, and his dad was a coach as mine had been. I was fortunate to have a great new job with a close, supportive friend during this tumultuous time. Jim seemed to be doing quite well under the circumstances. His T-cell count (the number used to determine the "bad" cancer cells) was improving, and he was doing well at work.

My mother flew down to North Carolina to stay with him and told me that one day as Jim was heading out the door to play golf, he said, "I really feel good. I just can't believe I'm as sick as they say I am, feeling this way." People who saw him on TV during this period would say to me, "I thought your brother was sick, but he looks great on TV." And he did. He had lost a little weight, he was tanned, and he looked, well, healthy. His public persona didn't do much to change that impression. He was glib about his situation, made jokes about it, and was still quick-witted and sharp. People commented that he didn't lose his hair after chemo; he said he had the world's toughest hair, industrial strength hair. They commented on his weight loss. He said he was now lighter and quicker. There wasn't an announcer in the country who could get around him. Funny Jim. Vintage Jim. For one brief, amazing moment I actually believed he was going to beat it. Everything he said would happen, had happened. Mom was feeling well, I had a new coaching job, and he was still doing a great job on TV with the chemotherapy seemingly having a positive effect.

In fact, while Jim's "bad" cancer-cell count had improved, it was still nowhere near the "remission" stage. When the cancer had spread as much as it had in his body, the chemo would reduce the cell count for a while, but then. . . . And so, at Christmas time, he got worse.

I went to see him and was still amazed at his determination. He was still working, trying to play golf, and going out with friends. We laughed at *Whose Line Is It, Anyway?* and went out to eat cheese-steak sandwiches with his good friend Frank McCann. And we talked. It was uplifting just to be around him, even in this state. I asked him how he was able to keep going, and he said it was simple. He said when you get sick, you have a choice. You can either wait to die or you can choose to live, and he was choosing to live. He also said he felt a sense of obligation to other cancer patients, that when he missed being on a show at ESPN the switchboard would be flooded with calls from cancer patients wanting to know if he was OK. He said many patients were getting inspiration and encouragement in their own battles against the disease by watching him in his struggle, and he wasn't about to let those people down.

Those two simple thoughts, "choose life" and "inspire others," were at the core of all Jim did for the rest of his life, and in a sense were really what defined him *all* of his life. Given a choice in any situation, he chose to "live," to dance every dance and experience life to its fullest. And he also felt a great obligation to those who depended on him, whose friendship and loyalty he treasured.

Oddly enough, that night we went out for steak sandwiches, while great fun, indicated to me that something had changed. The last time I had been with him, Jim took great pains to avoid red meat. This was because one theory about "naturalistic" healing of cancer had any red meat high on its list of no-nos. Jim had been very careful about what he ate, and talked at length about different types of food and how they were important. Now here he was eating a steak sandwich simply because he felt like having one—and that told me something had changed. When we got home he told me the tumors had spread. He showed them to me on his head and shoulders, let me touch them, in fact. And I wanted to. I wanted to feel those hideous monsters that were ruining our world with my own hands. And I began to see that it was a fight he wasn't going to win.

The last months became a kind of miasma of blurred visions and landscapes, frantic at some levels and torturous in their slow motion in others. Jim had changed treatment facilities to Duke University Hospital, and because of that Coach Mike Krzyzewski was a frequent visitor, almost on a daily basis toward the end. Said Krzyzewski:

> The last few months all the "protection levels" were gone. During those last times, you could say anything. It is difficult to

find someone in your life that has lived so similar an experience. I found that in Jim and he in me. Ethnic backgrounds, playing, coaching, the ACC . . . I considered him as smart and as good as myself, and I think he felt the same. I really felt we got to the highest level of confiding in one another. It was a gradual thing, just from the frequency of contact. I mean, he knew he was going to die, and there was no layer of pretense left.

Make no mistake, there were times when I was coaching that I hated Jimmy. I would think, "Look at that flashy SOB. I want to kick his ass." Competitive, and he was the same with me. But it was never really a bad relationship, and it really started to get close when he began doing TV. Then as these visits in the hospital picked up, honestly, we didn't even want other people in the room. It was like coaching when you have a really good point guard, and you start talking, and he finishes your sentences for you. That is how close we got at the end.

And we talked about anything and everything. Basketball, sure, but so much more. I got some great insight into how he felt about cancer at this time. I mean, he was dumbfounded that people wouldn't try *anything* to try to beat it, and I came to agree with him. He felt, hey, it's my life . . . just give me something. Let's try anything. If you're telling me I am going to die, I should have the right to try anything I choose. And he was amazed those things couldn't happen.

I think it pissed him off so much that he came up with the idea for his foundation. You know how coaches are when we get mad. We say, "Damn it, we're gonna win! We're gonna find some way to get this done." And I'm sure that was the way the V Foundation started, at least for Jim. It was anger and frustration about not being able to try things to make a difference, and the coach in him that wanted to organize something to find a way to win.

Still, there were a lot of things for Jim to do. He began to paint, since he never could sleep anyway, and even less so now. Late at night, with the house quiet, he would paint things his family liked. His first effort was a brown boat he tried to copy from the cover picture on the box of paints he bought. He did paintings for Pam, pictures for his kids, friends. It was great therapy for him, but it also showed that in the midst of his sickness he could still make life better for others, more fun, more special. Soon after the brown boat was finished, he invited family and friends to his house for the unveiling and for a "Meet the Artist" night. He wore a beret and sunglasses, like I guess he thought an artist should, and had the picture on an easel covered by a sheet. While his guests nibbled cheese and sipped wine, he talked about his "struggles as an artist," regaling his audience with tales about his difficulties before he found his "voice" and his "vision." Then he unveiled the painting, to resounding applause from the crowd, and insisted that everyone pose individually for a photo with him and the picture, but only if they agreed to wear sunglasses and a beret. Laughter, stories, warmth, joy . . . and all the magic came from one man. The man dying of cancer.

A few weeks later I spoke with Jim on the phone and he told me he was to receive the Arthur Ashe Award for Courage at the first ESPY Awards ceremony at Radio City Music Hall in New York City. ESPN does not lend its name to poorly executed projects, and my guess is that the ESPYs would still have become the success they are without Jim's speech. But I'm also pretty sure it got the ESPYs some attention a little more quickly; it gave the "light" evening a big dose of substance when Jim took the podium and made his "Don't Give Up . . . Don't Ever Give Up" speech. That speech endures and is the single most requested item at the V Foundation. (You can read the speech in its entirety in Appendix 1 of this book.)

Shortly after that speech, I gave my own tribute to Jim on my weekly cable TV show, which I hosted as part of my coaching duties at St. Mary's College:

My Brother, My Friend, My Hero

I have been coaching basketball for 15 years, and for most of that time my brother Jim, who is battling cancer, has been a nationally prominent figure. I have been constantly asked about Jim, and while I have always enjoyed it, my answers have often been flip attempts at humor, often paraphrasing my brother's own response early in his career about his resemblance to Joe Namath. Jim would say, "He's rich so people say he's ruggedly handsome. I'm poor so people say I have a big nose." Or, my own response to "I'm a big fan of Jimmy V's—you look just like him," would be, "Talk about your left-handed compliments!"

All of us in NCAA Division III basketball wear many different hats. In addition to my coaching, I teach a course in the sociology of sport. One of the things we discuss is that it seems that America, for whatever reason, has lost its heroes. I feel I have been blessed because my hero is my brother. I am certainly proud of his accomplishments: winning the national championship and the ACC championship, and going into broadcasting and winning an ACE award in his first year, among the many other significant things he achieved. But being a hero is not about what you do, it's about who you are, and from the unique perspective of the only "little brother" Jim Valvano has ever had, I can tell you something about who he is to me.

People always ask, "What do you guys talk about—basketball?" Sure we do, about 2 percent of the time. It would be easier to discuss what we *don't* talk about, or more accurately, what he has not taught me about. I have seen compassion, generosity, and tolerance in my brother's world, and have learned about those qualities through him. I have seen excitement too. My brother's zest for life is boundless, and has instilled in me an appreciation for the wonders of the world. Isn't it funny, I have always thought, how it is the same world that surrounds all of us, yet some people find it so fascinating, some so awful. It is my brother's life that has shown me how to find the wonder of it all.

And God knows he has taught me—yes, taught me—laughter. It really is in the most unusual of places, if you know where to look. James Thomas Anthony Valvano knew where to look. He taught me—seemingly at the most improbable of times— to be sure to look for the laugh. At the very least, you often get a smile. And he taught me about love. Most recently, he taught me—and all of us—a new lesson. It is called courage. It's one of the most difficult lessons I've ever had to learn.

I wish I could help him fight the fight as he has helped me fight my fights all these years. Jim, not an hour goes by where the people close to you don't wish there was something they could do to ease the pain.

Writer John Feinstein had a chance to reconcile with Jimmy during this difficult time:

Jim basically didn't talk to me after I wrote what I did when he was going through his rough times at N.C. State, and I think we were fairly close before that. It had been well over two years now, and I am very glad about our last meeting. The last game he did was the Duke–Carolina game in Chapel Hill. I was doing the game for radio. I was heading past the TV location courtside, and there was a lot of security around, since there were so many people who wanted to talk to Jim, wish him well.

I saw him and kind of waved at him, surrounded by like six security people who looked like they would just as soon shoot you as talk to you. Jimmy calls to me, and tells the security guys to let me through. I sit down, and he just says, "John, how are you doing?" making small talk. Then he looked at me and said, "I just want you to know I know why you wrote what you did. I understand why you did it. I don't agree with everything you wrote, but I know that in your case you felt you had to do it because it was your job."

I said, "That means a lot to me . . . because that *is* what I was doing." I told him, "You know how I feel about you." I said, "Unlike some people, I liked you *before* you had cancer." He just cracked up, and I gave him a little hug. . . .

God, he was so frail at that point, and I went on my way. That was the last time I saw him and that remains very important to me.

Jim was trying to get closure with a lot of people but, quite simply, his life had touched so many others in so many ways that it was difficult to get to them all. He had our mother, who was still trying to recover from heart bypass surgery, and his daughters, all working practically full-time helping him try to answer the thousands of notes and cards coming in. He wanted to answer them all, and to this day I have people who come up to me and say, "You know, I wrote your brother a few times, and every time I did, I got an answer. I never met him, but he always responded." That was very important to Jim. It was not unusual to go into his study and see two whole mailbags filled with notes and cards waiting for a reply. In the end, it became impossible to keep up.

In April of 1993 Jim left his house for the last time to go to Duke University Hospital.

And so, there I was staring at him. Trying to reconcile the guilt I was feeling. How could I feel what I was feeling about this man who I loved so much? How could I wish that he would die? Why wasn't I around more? I seemed to remember every second we had spent together over the last year, even every visit by phone, every time I saw him on TV, all of it . . . and it wasn't enough. I felt there should have been more, I should have done more. Closed eyes had replaced Jim's blank stare but it looked nothing like restful sleep. With the commotion of the arrival of my wife and young son, attention was diverted down the hall for a bit, but now in the room were Pam, Nicole (who was holding and kissing her father's hand), and me and my wife, Darlene.

Suddenly, Jim opened his eyes; he looked around the room and ultimately right at Pam, and then closed his eyes again. But this time he stopped breathing. It's so odd to remember what happened next. Even though we all knew the end had come, we ran around, scrambling to find a nurse. Darlene was closest to the door, so she raced down the hall. A flurry of activity . . . a nurse, two nurses . . .

Anyone who has endured the pain of watching a cancer patient wither away knows the value, trust, compassion, support, and love you find in the nursing staff. It was somehow appropriate that with all the wonderful doctors who were there round the clock for us, it was one of the nurses who looked up and said with a choked voice, "He's gone."

The rest of the family was immediately in the room. My mother, Jamie, Lee Ann. My brother Nick had just gone back to his hotel to change clothes and came in moments later. I think God did a good thing in not letting him have to see his little brother die. And I thank God for allowing my mother the momentary diversion of her grandson's arrival so she didn't have to see her son die either. Pam needed to be there for her husband, Nicole did as the oldest daughter, and I did since Jim was my older brother. Darlene was there for me. I believe God arranged the bedside scene perfectly.

There were many people in the hall who had been visiting throughout the day. We felt it appropriate that these great friends, tireless in their support, get a chance to say a last good-bye. Mike Krzyzewski, Frank McCann, so many other friends came in and cried with us for a few minutes, and then gracefully made their exits.

I don't know why, but I thought we should say something. I didn't know what, but something more than just good-bye. I remembered a poem Jim loved, a poem by Edna St. Vincent Millay called "First Fig," and through blurred eyes, I recited it:

> My candle burns at both ends
> It will not last the night;
> But ah, my foes and oh, my friends,
> It gives a lovely light.

The hospital staff arranged for us to go out a back door because even though it had been only about 30 minutes since Jim died, there was already a media throng at the door. We slipped quietly out the back and as I got in my car with Darlene, my son, and Darlene's mother, I turned the radio on. The host said, "We're all saddened by the passing of former N.C. State Coach Jim Valvano. This next song is for him."

It was Michael Jackson's "Gone Too Soon." It was then that the tears really started. He was gone . . . and it was much too soon.

13

THE GIFTS OF JIMMY V

HE WAS GONE, BUT AS WITH ANY LOVED ONE, HIS SPIRIT LIVED ON, AND the gifts he gave lived on in the lives of those he had touched.

As part of the interviewing process for this book, several of Jim's closest friends were asked what specific words they would use to describe him, and why. There were actually 58 separate words selected in all, but the words chosen most often, in descending order of frequency, were: *passionate, charismatic, funny, intelligent, complex, compassionate, fun, creative, loyal, egotistical, brilliant, emotional, driven, enigmatic, inspiring, analytical, competitive, tormented, insecure, disciplined, naïve, high-strung, driven, curious, brave,* and *unforgettable.* Said John Feinstein:

> I chose the word *brilliant* because I already told you how I thought Jim was as bright as anyone I knew. And he was curious, because it seemed to me he was interested in everything. I remember he was reading a book about perestroika while he was flying all over the place in 1987, and he said to me, "John, the Soviet Union is gonna be gone within three years." He was right, and he knew he was right. Because of all he had an interest in and all he could do, he always had a sense of "What am I going to do when I grow up?" Because of that I also chose the word *tormented.*
>
> He had won the National Championship, he had proved he could do TV, speak, make money, if he chose. Yet he wasn't able to get complete satisfaction from any of them, so he was always looking for the next challenge. He could never find

peace. Cancer gave his life direction. It gave his life meaning, but a very different kind of meaning.

When I heard that he had died, I was on my way to teach a class at Duke, and all we did that session was talk about Jim. I asked the class what words they would use to describe his life. Many of them are what you might expect—*passion, emotion, energy*—but what came out of it was that here was a guy with seemingly unlimited potential, unlimited promise *as a person*. The last year of his life we saw him fulfill that potential in ways he hadn't before. Because of that, while he leaves a legacy as a successful coach and broadcaster, it will be those last 10 months that we will remember and will ultimately be the legacy of Jim Valvano.

Said my brother Nick:

> I don't think there is any question that Jim was insecure. He felt that at any moment, all of it could go away, and he would regret not having done some things when he had the chance. I think he was naïve too, because he really could not believe some times there were other people with their own agendas out there. If he wanted to do something just because he wanted to do it, to experience it, he couldn't believe that people would not accept that at face value. Some couldn't because they didn't want to, and Jim had a hard time believing that.

Said Bob Costas:

> He had a certain life force, where you felt more alive just to be around him. He was filled with vitality and charisma, but also a certain vulnerability that made him more appealing. There was something lovable about him, and it was because he always had that human quality.

I think it's clear that while the words are not exactly the same, Jim was regarded by those whose lives he touched as funny, fun-loving, smart, curious, driven, and complex. He had charisma and presence and could motivate and inspire. He made mistakes, and he could be tough, demanding, and very competitive. He ultimately chose a very busy, full life, one with all sorts of challenges that he thought he could meet. He had a healthy ego too, of course. Of that there is little doubt.

But when you examine the source of that strong ego, you find the ultimate source of Jim's gift. When Jim was in your life, you looked at this guy touching and changing people from all walks of life, achieving and striving and growing, and through it all you got the feeling he was saying, "You should be doing all this too! You can do all of this. You can do whatever you choose to. I believe in that, and I am walking proof." He never forgot the power that came from the knowledge that his father believed in him. Jim wanted to pass that faith on to others.

Typical of Jim, though, even that wasn't enough. He wanted all of us to go and find others in our lives who could be reenergized by the knowledge that someone believed in them. He challenged all of us to be the kind of "rekindlers" that Albert Schweitzer talked about. His gift was to instill the belief in ourselves that we could do just that because he had, and he was very human indeed.

As Geoff Mason says, Jim was brave; but to him that was simply a choice. It was as if he said, "I am going to simply keep living. I will live my life—really live it—until I am no longer alive to do it." It was just that simple. Easy, no. Simple, yes.

And so, hopefully, Jim's "gift" lives on. As he loved to say all the time, God must have loved ordinary people because he made so many of us; yet every day ordinary people do extraordinary things. You can be that person. All of us work in different communities, but Jim's message would be a simple one: make a difference in *yours*. You can, we all can, and we all should.

Let me ask you what I used to ask my players every year after Jim passed away. How many of you are afraid of dying of polio? Of course, no one raises their hand. Polio? Who gets polio now? But if you had asked that question 50 or 60 years ago, the response would have been entirely different. Damn right people were scared of polio, my mother *had* polio when she was pregnant with Jimmy, and most people knew someone who had it or a family who had lost someone to it. Yet it has been eliminated from our world in less than a lifetime.

Why don't we think we can do that with cancer? When did we stop believing that we could actually *win* the fight with cancer? Why don't we believe that with *anything* of importance in our lives? That is Jim's message, and his gift: that we can make a difference every day in the things we care about most.

Find out what's important in your life. You're the only person who can answer that. Believe that you can make a difference in making it happen, and then work your tail off to make it so. Be enthusiastic about it, about your life! "Nothing great has ever been achieved without enthusiasm," said Ralph Waldo Emerson. Love the important people in your life, and let them know it, and remember to have a laugh along the way. *That* is the "Gift of Jimmy V," and it lives on, and will live on, forever.

Appendix I

THE ESPYS SPEECH

ON MARCH 4, 1993, JIM VALVANO WAS AWARDED THE INAUGURAL Arthur Ashe Award for Courage at the American Sports Awards, known as the ESPYs. This was his acceptance speech:

Thank you. Thank you very much. Thank you. That's the lowest I've ever seen Dick Vitale since the owner of the Detroit Pistons called him in and told him he should go into broadcasting.

I can't tell you what an honor it is to even be mentioned in the same breath with Arthur Ashe. This is something I certainly will treasure forever. But, as it was said on the tape, and I also don't have one of those things going with the cue cards, so I'm going to speak longer than anybody else has spoken tonight. That's the way it goes. Time is very precious to me. I don't know how much I have left and I have some things that I would like to say. Hopefully, at the end, I will have said something that will be important to other people too.

But I can't help it. Now I'm fighting cancer, everybody knows that. People ask me all the time about how you go through your life and how's your day, and nothing is changed for me. As Dick said, I'm a very emotional and passionate man. I can't help it. That's being the son of Rocco and Angelina Valvano. It comes with the territory. We hug, we kiss, we love. When people say to me how do you get through life or each day, it's the same thing. To me, there are three things we all should do every day. We should do this every day of our lives.

Number one is laugh. You should laugh every day. Number two is think. You should spend some time in thought. Number three is, you should have your emotions moved to tears, could be happiness or joy. But think about it. If you laugh, you think, and you cry, that's a full day. That's a heck of a day. You do that seven days a week, you're going to have something special.

I rode on the plane up today with Mike Krzyzewski, my good friend and a wonderful coach. People don't realize he's 10 times a better person than he is a coach, and we know he's a great coach. He's meant a lot to me in these last five or six months with my battle. But when I look at Mike, I think, we competed against each other as players, I coached against him for 15 years, and I always have to think about what's important in life to me are these three things: where you started, where you are, and where you're going to be. Those are the three things that I try to do every day. When I think about getting up and giving a speech, I can't help it. I have to remember the first speech I ever gave.

I was coaching at Rutgers University, that was my first job, oh, that's wonderful [he reacts to applause from audience] and I was the freshman coach. That's when freshmen played on freshman teams, and I was so fired up about my first job. I see Lou Holtz here. Coach Holtz, who doesn't like the very first job they had? The very first time you stood in the locker room to give a pep talk. That's a special place—the locker room—for a coach to give a talk. So my idol as a coach was Vince Lombardi, and I read this book called *Commitment to Excellence* by Vince Lombardi. And in the book, Lombardi talked about the first time he spoke before his Green Bay Packers team in the locker room, when they were perennial losers. I'm reading this and Lombardi said he was thinking should it be a long talk, or a short talk? But he wanted it to be emotional, so it would be brief. So here's what I did. Normally you get in the locker room, I don't know, 25 minutes, a half hour before the team takes the field, you do your little *X*s and *O*s, and then you give the great Knute Rockne talk. We all do. Speech No. 84. You pull them right out, you get ready. You get your squad ready. Well, this is the first one I ever gave, and I read this thing. Lombardi, what he said was he didn't go in, he waited. His team wondering, where is he? Where is this great coach? He's not there. Ten minutes, he's still not there. Three minutes before they could take the field, Lombardi comes in, bangs the door open, and I think you all remember what a great presence he had, great presence. He walked in and he walked back and forth, like this, just walked, staring at the players. He said, "All eyes on me." I'm reading this in this book. I'm getting this picture of Lombardi before his first game, and he said, "Gentlemen, we will be successful this year if you can focus on three things and three things only: your family, your religion, and the Green Bay Packers." They knocked the wall down and the rest was history. I said, that's beautiful. I'm going to do that. Your family, your religion, and Rutgers basketball. That's it. I had it. Listen, I'm 21 years old. The kids I'm coaching are 19, and I'm going to be the greatest coach in the world, the next Lombardi. I'm practicing outside of the locker room and the managers tell me you got to go in. Not yet, not yet . . . family, religion, Rutgers basketball. All eyes on me. I got it, I got it. Then finally he said, three minutes, I said fine. True story. I go to knock the doors open just like Lombardi. Boom! They don't open. I almost broke my arm. Now I was down, the players were looking. Help the coach out. Help him out. Now I did like Lombardi; I walked back and forth, and I was going like that with my arm getting the feeling back in it. Finally I said, "Gentlemen, we'll be successful this year if you can focus on three things, and three things only: your family, your religion, and the Green Bay Packers," I told them. I did that. I remember that. I remember where I came from.

It's so important to know where you are. I know where I am right now. How do you go from where you are to where you want to be? I think you have to have an enthusiasm for life. You have to have a dream, a goal. You have to be willing to work for it.

I talked about my family, my family's so important. People think I have courage. The courage in my family are my wife, Pam, my three daughters, here, Nicole, Jamie, Lee Ann, my mom, who's right here too. That screen is flashing up there 30 seconds, like I care about that screen right now, huh? I got tumors all over my body. I'm worried about some guy in the back going "30 seconds"? You got a lot, hey *va fa napoli*, buddy. You got a lot.

I just got one last thing. I urge all of you, all of you, to enjoy your life, the precious moments you have. To spend each day with some laughter and some thought, to get your emotions going. To be enthusiastic every day and as Ralph Waldo Emerson said, "Nothing great could be accomplished without enthusiasm," to keep your dreams alive in spite of problems, whatever you have. The ability to be able to work hard for your dreams to come true, to become a reality.

Now I look at where I am now and I know what I want to do. What I would like to be able to do is spend whatever time I have left and to give, and maybe, some hope to others. The Arthur Ashe Foundation is a wonderful thing, and AIDS is, the amount of money pouring in for AIDS is not enough, but is significant. But what if I told you it's 10 times the amount that goes in for cancer research? What if I also told you that 500,000 people will die this year of cancer? And also tell you that one in every four will be afflicted with this disease, and yet somehow, we seem to have put it in a little bit of the background. I want to bring it back on the front table. We need your help. I need your help. We need money for research. It may not save my life. It may save my children's lives. It may save someone you love and ESPN has been so kind to support me in this endeavor and allow me to announce tonight that with ESPN's support, which means what?—their money and their dollars and their helping me—we are starting the Jimmy V Foundation for cancer research. And its motto is "Don't give up, don't ever give up." That's what I'm going to try to do every minute that I have left. I will thank God for the day and the moment I have. If you see me, smile and give me a hug. That's important to me too. But try if you can to support, whether it's AIDS or the cancer foundation, so that someone else might survive, might prosper, and might actually be cured of this dreaded disease. I can't thank ESPN enough for allowing this to happen. I'm going to work as hard as I can for cancer research and hopefully, maybe, we'll have some cures and some breakthroughs. I'd like to think I'm going to fight my brains out to be back here again next year for the Arthur Ashe recipient. I want to give it next year!

I know I gotta go, I gotta go, and I got one last thing and I said it before and I want to say it again. Cancer can take away all my physical abilities. It cannot touch my mind, it cannot touch my heart, and it cannot touch my soul. And those three things are going to carry on forever.

I thank you and God bless you all.

Appendix II

THE V FOUNDATION

THERE WAS SUCH A HUGE VOID CREATED IN SO MANY OF OUR LIVES with Jim's passing that the whole year after was a whirlwind of activity as people tried to channel their grief, pain, loss, and helplessness into something positive. For many, that outlet became the V Foundation.

A lot happened that first year, starting from scratch and building from the ground up, but what a team we had to work with! There was Coach Mike Krzyzewski, broadcasters John Saunders and Leslie Visser, then president of ESPN (and now president of ABC television) Steve Bornstein, entertainer Bill Cosby, my brother's old roommate, Bob Lloyd, who had gone on to quite a career in business, former Duke Coach Bucky Waters, ESPN executive producer Geoff Mason, head of the Washington Speakers' Bureau Harry Rhoads, former N.C. State star Dereck Whittenburg, world-class doctors from Sloan Kettering and Duke University Medical Center like Bob Bast and Joe Moore, as well as family members Nick, Pam, and myself. At the beginning, we had no office, no staff, no logo, no stationery, nothing!

In 2001, we will go over the $20 million mark, not bad for a foundation less than nine years old. It has built the Jim Valvano Day Hospital at Duke Medical Center and funded over 130 scientists across the country, who are doing cutting-edge research to achieve breakthroughs in the fight, some with amazingly promising results. It has helped establish a summer scholars program at Hipple Cancer Research Center in Dayton, Ohio. The board has grown to include the likes of Dick Vitale, George Bodenheimer (the current president of ESPN), Kay Yow (the hugely successful women's basketball coach at N.C. State), Phil Knight (founder and chairman of Nike), and business leaders like Mike MacDonald of Xerox and Bob Nakisone, former CEO of Toys "R" Us.

And of course there are the ancillary events and organizations that have evolved from the Foundation over the last several years. There's the annual Jimmy V Celebrity Golf Classic, which is the brainchild of Jim's friend Frank McCann. Held every August in Cary, North Carolina, and staffed by almost 1,000 volunteers, this event now raises over $1 million each year. The Jimmy V Basketball Classic has attracted some of the nation's best college teams to the Meadowlands for a doubleheader every December, and it will soon be joined by the Jimmy V Women's Basketball Classic, which will debut in North Carolina in 2002. The ESPYs have continued to showcase ESPN's continuing commitment to the V Foundation, and the V Wine Celebration in Napa Valley, California, is a new event that has been a tremendous success on every level and has proved to be an excellent fund-raiser as well.

Speaking of ESPN, their commitment to the Foundation displays a burning passion to lead the way in the fight against cancer. From Steve Bornstein and George Bodenheimer down through the ranks of on-air personalities and staffers at every level, the company is filled with people who give their time, talent, and energy in the great struggle to find a cure for this dreaded disease. The list of people is far too long to mention each by name, but on behalf of the Foundation, I would like to say a hearty and heartfelt "thank you" to each and every one of you. May God bless you as we continue in this great effort together.

For more information about the V Foundation, call 1-800-4JIMMYV or log on to www.jimmyv.org.

Appendix III

TRIBUTES TO JIMMY V

THERE WERE THREE COLUMNS WRITTEN UPON JIM'S DEATH THAT STOOD out from the rest in my opinion. Of course, there were many fine and emotional things written about Jim's life and death; but these, I feel, were the best of the best. John Feinstein's column appeared in *Basketball America*; Tony Kornheiser's column appeared in the *Washington Post*; and Mike Lupica's column appeared in the *New York Daily News*.

Destroyed By Success, Resurrected By Death
by John Feinstein

Reprinted from *Basketball America*, June 1993.
Used with permission.

When death touches us, when someone we loved, or liked, or perhaps simply respected dies, it is only natural to pause and think about the life they lived. It is just as natural to think about our own lives, because the death of a friend or relative inevitably causes each of us to think, at least for a moment, about our own mortality.

This is especially true when the death is premature, when it comes suddenly or much too soon. Jim Valvano was 47 on the morning of April 28th, and there is no doubting the fact that his death came much too soon, that his life, no matter how full it may have been, was far too short.

Since that morning, the clichés have poured from television sets and computers like this one, seamlessly: He was so full of life; he was a beautiful person; he was a symbol of courage; he brought joy to those around him. There is truth in each of those statements, but they are as empty as they are true. And they do nothing to make sense of the life Jim lived or the way he died.

Because the real truth is this: He was a man destroyed by success and resurrected by death. Those are harsh words, but they are written with a great deal of thought and with enormous sadness, because the tragic irony of Jim Valvano's life was that it was cancer that gave him the direction and focus that success could not.

We all remember 1983: Survive and Advance, The Dunk, the Sprint, and the joy that, it seemed then, would live forever. Valvano was his sport's brightest star, a brilliant young coach who had the genius of Knight and Smith without all the emotional baggage. He didn't throw chairs; he jumped on them so more people could hear him. He didn't need silly little mind games, just an audience.

And the world came and said, "We are your audience." The Sprint around The Pit became a marathon. He was 37 and he thought he had "done" coaching. He began searching for The Next Thing and in the process he destroyed himself professionally and personally, chasing every dollar, every camera, every speech, everything that wasn't coaching and wasn't his family. If Lorenzo Charles hadn't dunked that ball on that fateful night in Albuquerque, maybe coaching would still have been his passion. Instead, it became nothing more than a fallback when there weren't other things to do, and that approach ultimately led to his downfall and forced resignation at North Carolina State.

Valvano was far from unique. There isn't a profession in the world that doesn't have a wunderkind who fell to earth because it was too much too soon. Anyone who has done what I do for more than 15 minutes knows the story of Bob Woodward and Carl Bernstein. After Watergate, Bernstein had "done" reporting. He began searching for a new challenge. He tried TV and writing novels and writing scripts and living in the fast lane. He ended up the butt of cruel jokes and grist for gossip mills.

Valvano was Bernstein. Albuquerque was Watergate. Twenty miles west on I-40, Valvano's lifelong rival and late-life friend, Mike Krzyzewski, became Woodward. To Woodward, Watergate was a great learning experience for a reporter. He was a reporter before Watergate and a reporter after Watergate. He never doubted that for a second. He has continued to write important books since Watergate, still growing in the job even now at age 50.

When Krzyzewski won a national championship, his first thoughts were not about what to do next but about how to win again, how to do a better job the next year than he had done that year. Dean Smith is different than Krzyzewski, but he has always had that hunger, that need to prove himself again and again.

Once upon a time, Valvano used to sit up late at night and talk about Smith and Krzyzewski. He said over and over that he knew he could never coach for 30 years, that he couldn't see dragging himself into teenagers' homes and into practice when he was 60. Or, for that matter, 50. So he searched. He tried TV and radio and motivational speaking. He tried being an entrepreneur, selling everything from posters to statues to blue jeans. He tried being an athletic director and being a stand-up comedian.

Unlike Bernstein, he was good at almost everything he tried because he was so damned smart he figured things out much faster than the rest of us. But he never found the answers or an answer. He never figured out what he wanted to be if he wasn't going to be a coach.

There were times when he would look wistfully down the road at Krzyzewski and say, "That's where I should have gone." Eventually, he came to love N.C. State but to him, Duke, the academic school, would have been the perfect fit because underneath the one liners and the changing defenses was a scholar. He quoted from literature—the real stuff, not sportswriting—all the time, and he often talked about how much he would have loved coaching Duke kids in the unique atmosphere of Cameron Indoor Stadium.

Everyone believes the grass is greener on the other side of the fence. The sad part about Valvano's wandering eye is that the challenge he searched the world for was right under his nose, so close that he looked right past it.

Getting 95% of your players to graduate from Duke is not that difficult a feat. In fact, Krzyzewski often points out that any Duke coach who falls very far below that level won't be a Duke coach for too long. What's more, convincing basketball players with brains to go to Duke—or North Carolina—isn't exactly as difficult as splitting the atom. Both have great campuses, impeccable academic reputations and superb basketball traditions that seem to grow each year.

But building a program at State that would win year in and year out *and* graduate players *and* consistently bring in bright, articulate youngsters . . . now there was a challenge. Certainly State takes a back seat to no one when it comes to basketball tradition. But academically it has always been viewed—fairly or unfairly—as a cow college, a poor relation to its sister campus in Chapel Hill, a school that couldn't begin to compete with Carolina or Duke in either academics or athletics.

After Albuquerque, Valvano was the most visible and popular basketball coach in the game. There were very few players in the country who would not, at the very least, have considered playing for him. Imagine what might have happened if Valvano had focused his eloquence and his energy on convincing players like Christian Laettner, Danny Ferry, J. R. Reid, Kenny Anderson, Bryant Stith, Eric Montross, James Forrest, Bobby Hurley, Cory Alexander and Travis Best—to name a few who played in the ACC—that they should come and play for him. Would he have gotten all of them? Certainly not. Would he have gotten some of them? You bet.

And then he might have achieved something really special, building a program at State that could stand side by side with Duke and Carolina, on *and* off the court. Instead, he went searching, the program ran amok and we all know what happened. Valvano went off to television, where he was very good and very funny and it was all very empty because he was capable of so much more.

And then came cancer. Somehow, from the moment the doctors told him what he had and how serious it was, Jim

Valvano finally found The Next Thing. He knew his time was limited, but he desperately wanted to make his death mean something. And he did. The last 10 months, painful as they were for his family and those who cared about him, were the best 10 months. He dreamed the dream one more time. He was brilliant and he was brave and he left an important legacy: The Jimmy V Cancer Fund. He reminded people who had forgotten in the wake of the horrors of AIDS that cancer still kills far too often.

And, in the two extraordinary speeches he made near the end, he left us with memories of just how remarkable he could be when he really put his mind to something.

Even so, there is sadness because he had so little time to make that final mark. It was John Greenleaf Whittier who once wrote, "For of all sad words of tongue or pen, the saddest are these: It might have been."

For a long time, after The Dunk, those words applied to Jim Valvano. But in those last 10 months, there were no mights or maybes. There *was*. And because he *was* a symbol of hope and awareness and courage, he left us with more than memories. In the end he left us with a beginning.

When I think of him in the future, that fact will make me smile. Even through my tears.

Measured Not by His Wins, But by Our Loss
by Tony Kornheiser

Reprinted from the *Washington Post*. Used with permission.

A letter arrived the other day, coincidentally, from my friend Bob Valvano, Jimmy's younger brother. Bob enclosed a sentiment Jimmy often quoted, Albert Schweitzer's saying: "In everyone's life, at some time, our inner fire goes out. It is then burst into flame by an encounter with another human being. We should all be thankful for those people who rekindle the inner spirit."

Jimmy Valvano was one of those who consistently rekindled our inner spirits. He was so magnetic and so hilarious and so full of life that you simply could not help but be happy around him. He was not merely a breath of fresh air—he was the Santa Ana wind. With his death yesterday it's already beginning to feel stuffy around here.

I've known him almost 20 years, dating back to when he was a coach at small schools such as Bucknell and Johns Hopkins. He'd talk about going to a coaching convention and introducing himself to Dick Motta. "I'm Jim Valvano. I coach at Johns Hopkins." Motta, who was a big-time NBA coach, looked down his nose and said, "Oh yeah? What do you coach, pediatrics?" A few years later Valvano had moved to Iona, and he returned to the convention and reintroduced himself to Motta. "I'm Jim Valvano. Iona College." Motta looked at this baby-faced kid and said, "Pretty young to own your own school."

Valvano loved telling these stories; he loved making himself the butt of the joke. Like whenever people mentioned he looked like Joe Namath, Jimmy would say, "Yeah, but when you look at Namath, you say he's ruggedly handsome; when you look at me, you say he's got a big nose."

Ten years ago this month Valvano won the NCAA championship in Albuquerque. Sixteen years in the business and boom, he's an overnight sensation. Ten years ago this week I went down to Raleigh to spend a couple of days with him. The deal was: He'd make me laugh, and I'd stay up all night, drinking wine and singing oldies with him, like he used to do at Joey DeFunzo's Railroad Inn in new Rochelle, near Iona, when he'd stand on the table and do "Runaround Sue."

He meets me at the airport and tells me that the NCAA has put in a new rule to cut down on recruiting. "For thirty straight days a coach cannot leave campus. I tell my wife about it. I say, 'Pam, I'm gonna be home with you and the kids for thirty straight days and nights.' She can't believe it. For 16 years I've been out recruiting. She says, 'Thirty days and nights in a row? Are you sure?' I say, 'I'm sure.' She says, 'Okay, I want to make love 28 times.' I say, 'Fine. Put me down for 2.'"

Jimmy had just come from Washington, where he had met Ronald Reagan—a huge event in the life of "the son of Rocco and Angelina Valvano," as Valvano often identified himself when describing the wondrous things that had come his way.

"I mean, I'm thrilled. I'm so excited that on the plane up, when the stewardess asks if I want coffee, I say, 'Sure. By the way, I'm going to the White House to meet the president.' I tell the cabbie, 'White House. I'm going to meet the president.' So I get there, and somebody comes in and tells me the president will be there in five minutes. What the hell was I gonna say?' He'd better be, because if he's not, I'm Gonesville—I'm bolting this joint.' They could have told me, 'The president will be here in October,' and I'd have said, 'Fine, can I maybe get some food and a cot while I wait?'"

This was the time in his life when Jimmy was on top of the world. Later on there would be "hints and allegations," as Paul Simon would say, about shabby recruiting and insufficient academic attention. But you can go elsewhere for bad stuff. This is about the Jimmy Valvano I see when I close my eyes, the New York boy who went south and learned how to eat barbecue—and occasionally beat Carolina. "The first time I coach against Carolina, we lose by one. The second time, we're down one, we miss a shot at the buzzer to win. A few days later I get a letter from a State alum that says, 'Coach, I know you're new here, and I know you're trying. But I'm not sure you understand how we feel about losing to Carolina. I know where you live, and if you lose to them one more time, I'm going to come to your house and shoot your dog.' Most of the time you get a letter like that, the writer won't sign his name. But it's so intense down here, the guy not only signs his name—he gives his social security number and references! I write him back, and I say, 'Look, I don't want to lose to Carolina any more than you do. But I gotta tell you: I don't have a dog.' Next day, a UPS guy rings my doorbell and hands me a package. I open it. There's a dog inside with a note around its neck that says: 'Don't get too attached.'"

I shouldn't give you the impression that it was all jokes all the time. If you pressed Jimmy, he would be serious. He was troubled with the value system of a culture that paid its athletes and coaches so much more than its teachers and firemen. Oh, Jimmy took the money. He wasn't Mother Teresa. But he was leery of what the money might do to him and his family. It's one thing to enjoy big money. It's quite another to need it. "We were sitting at the pool the other day and my daughter was paged. 'Phone call for Nicole Valvano.' I looked at Pam and said, 'Pammy, did you hear that? Our daughter was just paged at the country club pool.' I want to grab her and take her back to Queens with me, and go to the Aquacade where I used to stand in line for half a day waiting my turn to be able to jump in the water. Now my kids are paged at the country club pool. But what do I do—do I make them have hardships because I did? I don't know what to tell you. The other day I flew cross-country, first class, and I was sitting next to a guy who was obviously used to flying first class, and the stewardess asked me if I wanted some caviar. I mean, caviar! The guy next to me has been on this flight before, and he says, 'Don't have it. It's not good caviar.' I don't ever want to say, 'The caviar isn't good.'"

There's an old saying about how you'd better be careful what you wish for, because you might get it. Valvano got it at 37. The big kahuna. The NCAA championship. It happened just like he thought it would, like he actually wrote down on a card while he was still in college: Start out as an assistant, get a head coaching job at a small school, move up to a bigger school, then get the big-time job, then, bang, win the national title. Said Jim: "And you know what? It happened. Isn't that amazing? Ha, ha, ha, ha. Amazing. And it happened *faster* than I'd written it down. It was supposed to happen eight, nine years from now."

He said that in late April of 1983. We were in his office at North Carolina State, with the NCAA net hanging on the wall, and the free T-shirts and free sneakers sticking out of boxes, and the congratulatory telegrams stacked up, and the phone constantly ringing, and the offers for cookbooks and speeches and TV gigs pouring in, and the financial planners and the guy with the idea for the restaurant and the shopping center waiting outside.

And I asked Jimmy: What happens next? Does it get better? Or, is this all there is? And he said, "I wonder about it. I'm 37 years old, and I've got so many years ahead of me. I'd like to talk to somebody about it. I'd like to sit with Dean. He's the best. He's in the Hall of Fame. What else can they do for him? Name the game after him? 'Dean, you've been doing this for 21 years at the highest level. What do you want now? Tell me, I'm 37. You've got me by 14, 15 years. How are the next 10 years? Give me a hint.'"

I was driving south on Connecticut Avenue yesterday a little after noon. I had the radio on, and I was listening to people talk about Jimmy Valvano and what a funny, warm, enthusiastic person he was. I heard someone say that Jimmy lived life so fully and with such passion that, even if he was only 47 when he died, he'd crammed about 97 years of life in. I thought: That's right, what a ride he had. And I shook my head softly, because I really figured that if anybody could beat this cancer, it was Jimmy.

On the other side of the divider, going north on Connecticut near East-West Highway, came a line of cars with their headlights on, a funeral procession. I counted the cars as they went by, and when they were gone I pulled over to the side of the road and began to cry.

Valhalla Gets a Head Coach
by Mike Lupica

Reprinted from the *New York Daily News*. Used with permission.

Jim Valvano saved the best of himself until last. He defined himself more eloquently during the last year of his life than he ever did on a sideline or in front of a microphone or with a joke. It turns out that Valvano's greatest victory came in the face of inevitable defeat, which arrived yesterday, because of cancer. He was 47 years old, and some finisher.

At the end, fighting the cancer, Valvano was all the majesty that sport is supposed to have, all the ways that sport is supposed to take the best from life, all the ways it is supposed to illuminate heart and courage and the refusal to give in to anything. Jim Valvano's best came when he didn't have a chance.

He came from Roosevelt Avenue in Corona, out from under the elevated tracks there. He came from Seaford High School and Rutgers University, and Johns Hopkins and Iona and North Carolina State. Valvano even came out of late-night places like Joey DeFunzo's Roadway Bar in New Rochelle, when he was the coach at Iona, and he was first on the map, a comer, and all the nights of his life were going to be filled with red wine and laughter, until the next game, and the next night.

Dick Vitale said yesterday that Jimmy V was at his best between 11:00 at night and 1:00 in the morning, and maybe he was. Until this last year, anyway, when he fought the cancer. Then it wasn't the late nights and it wasn't N.C. State beating Houston in the NCAA final of 1983. One of those old Greeks once said that the most acute tragedies strike remarkable men. Valvano, because of his public and passionate fight against cancer, finally became that kind of remarkable man. Before, he had only been a basketball star. There are plenty of those.

"Cancer cannot touch my heart, it cannot touch my mind, it cannot touch my soul," Valvano said at ESPN's ESPY Awards in early March, his voice and spirit filling the Paramount Theater that night the way music is supposed to fill that place, or laughter.

One more time, in a big room, Valvano transformed himself, either by magic or the force of his will, into Jimmy V. and, despite his pain, had them in the palm of his hand. It really was his last public appearance. Of course he left us all wanting more.

He was of New York, so many extended parts of it, born in Queens and raised on the Island, then college in New Jersey and his first important coaching break up there in New Rochelle. He loved the Garden. When he was at Iona, he used to tell me all the time that he was going to coach the Knicks someday. He told me the same thing at N.C. State.

There was the day in a hallway of the Carrier Dome in Syracuse, after State had been upset early in the NCAA tournament. The Knicks were looking for a coach. They would hire Rick Pitino in a few weeks, but not yet. Valvano wanted in. He was on the hustle, because he always was. Sometimes he went too fast and did not always look where he was going, and eventually that all caught up with him at N.C. State, and he was forced to leave there before his coaching time.

But on this day in Syracuse, Valvano grinned and said to me, "How come the Knicks don't call me?" Then he told a story he was always telling, about a day when he was Iona coach and there was some kind of press luncheon at the Garden. The late Sonny Werblin was running the place in those days. Valvano, unannounced, knocked on Werblin's door and said, "You don't know me, Mr. Werblin. My name is Jim Valvano, and I'm going to coach your basketball team someday."

He never did. He never got another coaching job after N.C. State, even though he came close with the Nets. Television made him a star all over again. He could have gone forever in television. He got cancer and yesterday he died.

I was with him after wins and losses along the way. I saw him after he won in Albuquerque in 1983, against the odds. I saw him after he lost to St. John's in the final of the West Regional one year, and another time after the refs made a terrible call in the tournament and he didn't upset Georgetown in the Meadowlands. He always found a way to get a laugh. He always had a line.

There was the time back in 1983 when they changed recruiting rules, and it was announced that coaches were now required to spend 30 consecutive days on campus at some point during college basketball's off-season.

"I tell Pam [his wife] I can be home with you and the kids for thirty straight days and nights," Valvano told his friend Tony Kornheiser of the *Washington Post*. "She can't believe it. For 16 straight years, I've been out recruiting. She listened to me and then she said, 'Thirty days and nights in a row? Are you sure?' I said, 'I'm sure.' She says, 'Okay, I want to make love 28 times.' I say, 'Fine. Put me down for 2.'"

He went to meet President Reagan after State won the championship. Reagan said to him, "Do you pronounce your name Val-VAH-no or Val-VAY-no?" Valvano told him it was Val-VAH-no. Then he said to the president, "How about you? Is it RAY-gan or REE-gan?"

He was as good coaching a single game of basketball as anyone I have ever seen. So he was much more than a gym rat hustler or the stand-up comedy king of basketball. He had a splendid gift for coaching. He was sure after 1983 that he would win another national championship. He never did, the way he never coached the Knicks. Maybe there would have been another coaching job. But he got cancer.

In these last months, Valvano's favorite quotation came from Albert Schweitzer, of all people. His brother Bobby had these words framed for him: "In everyone's life at some time our inner fire goes out. It is then burst into flame by an encounter with another human being. We should all be thankful for those people who rekindle the inner spirit."

We are thankful today for Jim Valvano. He was better known as Jimmy V. He was the son of Rocco and Angelina. He coached a little basketball once. He made his share of mistakes. He died a champion yesterday.

Index